Hey Friend.

This is not another networking book. This is not a stalking book. This is not a dating book. And this is not an outdated book.

This is a connecting book with 21st-century connection techniques for 21st-century peeps.

This is a connecting book to show you how to curate and cultivate connections.

This is a connecting book to teach you how to #friendwork. How to use your "whos" not your "dos." How to focus on the person not the profession. How to share stories not glories.

This is a connecting book written by me for you in a world plagued by no new friends, counting friends on one hand, transactional networking—and where talking via tech is preferred over in-person chats.

This is a connecting book to revive friendships because the art and science of making friends is dying.

This is a connecting book to change the world one connection at a time and make the world friendly again or at the very least friendlier than it's ever been.

This is a connecting book friend and you can learn more about the **Hey Friend Movement** *at* WWW.HEYFRIENDCO.COM *and me at* WWW.KEISHAMABRY.COM

Happy reading!

10/8/17

She,

Thanks so much for the
support. Happy connecting!

–Keisha

hey FRIEND

100 Ways to Connect with
100 People in 100 Days

Keisha Mabry

www.keishamabry.com

ISBN: 978-0-9985879-0-5

Cover and interior design by Kirsten O'Loughlin

Printed in the United States of America

For information regarding special discounts for bulk purchases, please email keisha@keishamabry.com or visit the Contact Us page at www.keishamabry.com.

This book is dedicated to my first friend—my mother.

And written in loving memory of my brother.

***Thank you both
for teaching me how to love.***

con·nect

/kənekt/

•

verb

1. to bring together or into contact so that a real or notional link is established.

2. to join together so as to provide access and communication.

3. to chat in person over coffee, lunch, dinner, brunch or various other means to share stories.

DISCLAIMER

This book is written like a conversation. Like a conversation you would have with me. Sometimes in conversation I say I am and other times I say I'm. Sometimes I say shoulda, woulda, coulda and gotta intentionally and other times I use slang. Sometimes I start sentences with ands and buts and other times I cuss—but not much, just a time or two. So expect all of these and expect a few grammar and punctuation mistakes too, because sometimes I do that in conversation too. And that's my truth.

CONTENTS

Be Entrepreneurial
Work. Work. Work. Work. Work.

The End

Foreword: My Story

(And yes this chapter is mandatory so read it or be confused—very, very confused—when you read the rest of the text.)

What's your story? These are the three words I ask everyone upon meeting them. These are the three words I use to break the ice. But most people look at me very puzzled when they hear these three words and instead of breaking the ice I freezer-burn it. After a few moments of silence the person standing or sitting in front of me usually responds with a question. And not just any question but the very same question. *"What's my story?"* they ask as they search their brains for words that sound profound. *"Yes. What's your story? Your passion? Your purpose? Who are you?"* I expound.

Silence. Crickets. Blank Stares. Confusion.

So used to answering the preferred networking question *what do you do*, they stand or sit in silence, crickets, blank stares and confusion. They stand or sit not knowing who they are. They stand or sit only knowing what they do.

What they do. Not who they are.

But I want to know their who not their do. We are much more than what we do so I choose not to ask this question. I choose to get to know their who—their story. I choose to connect. But so used to networking. So used to networking with dos, they don't know their whos, they don't know their stories, they don't know how to connect and the *what's your story?* question freezes them.

At first. It freezes them at first. BUT then they get excited and they unfreeze. In fact they melt from excitement. BECAUSE for once in their life someone has given them permission to not speak about work. For once in their life someone wants to know their who not their do. Who they are—their hopes, dreams, passions and hobbies—not what they do from 9 to 5 just to stay alive.

The next moment is MAGICAL. I stand or sit and listen as the person talks nonstop for the next three to five minutes. I learn about their journey to purpose, I learn about their true selves, I learn about the things that make their eyes well. I learn. I listen. I listen and learn. And after hearing their story of self, I share my own. I share my own and we connect. We don't network, we connect. We connect over a relational moment not a transactional one. We connect over whos not dos.

If and only if I feel energy, chemistry and synergy, and if and only if I plan to do something with their contact information—I will ask for it. "It" as in their email address and their phone number. Not sure if you caught that but I do not ask for "it" as in their business card. I despise business cards because most end up in a pile on my desk or stuffed in a pocket of my laptop bag. So I avoid them at all cost.

Instead, I ask for email addresses and phone numbers and then I enter both into my phone RIGHT NEXT to the contact information for the rest of my friends. Well actually, I don't enter anything. I hand my phone to my new friend and they enter it. Then immediately, as in while the person is still standing there, I reach out to my new friend via text or email to remind them of our connection and to schedule our next one. Sometimes we schedule our next connection right there on the spot. Most people keep their calendars on their phones these days, so if you can go ahead and schedule it—by all means schedule away. But if you can't schedule right then and there, make sure to schedule the very next day.

Occasionally, some peeps will still hand me their business cards anyway. They do this if they feel weird taking my phone or if we are in a fast-paced space and place where there's no time to waste like speed networking or twerking. And yes. I've met a few friends twerking. So if and when people hand me their card, I take it. I cringe slightly, but I take it and I do the same thing I just told you I do.

I enter their email addresses and phone numbers into my phone and then I text or email them the same day before I make it back home, to my hotel or wherever I'm staying. I like to reach out to my new friends as soon as I can in order to keep the connection going. A delayed connection can turn into a missed or forgotten connection, so I don't chance it.

On the flip side. If I do not feel energy, chemistry or synergy, I chat for a few minutes longer, politely excuse myself, thank them for their time, bid them a good day and go on about mine. But this looks different depending on where I am:

> *If I am at an event, I say, "It was so great meeting you. I'm going to head to the bar before it gets too packed. Thanks for the chat." Or. "It was so great meeting you. I am going to see*

who else I can meet, but I hope you have a nice night." Or.
"So great meeting you. I'm going to grab a bite to eat and try
to get a good seat. See you later."

If I'm out and about, I say, "I have to get back to work but I
hope you enjoy the rest of your day. It was so great meeting
you." Or. "It was so great meeting you. I need to run a few
errands before it gets too late. I hope you enjoy the rest of your
day." Or. "Great meeting you. I've had a long day and need a
pillow and a bed to touch my head. I hope you have a
good night."

I know what you're probably thinking—HOW RUDE in Stephanie's voice from *Full House*—but it's ok to walk away. It's ok not to exchange contact information with everyone you encounter. And it's ok not to have a stack of business cards in a pile on your desk or stuffed in your laptop bag to never be seen again. It's ok.

So yes. If there's no energy, chemistry or synergy, I walk away. I enjoy the magical moment for what it is—a magical moment—and I go on about my day. One must recognize that people are in our lives for a reason, season or lifetime and that's a-ok, so fix your face.

Well friend. The time has come to share my own story, the who beyond my do and the person behind my profession. So. Here it goes. Clears throat and takes sip < *insert a throat clear and a sipping sound here* >.

I am part Dora the Explorer, part Olivia Pope and part Curious George. I like to explore the world, solve problems, ask why and dress fly. Yes friend. I like to dress fly.

I live a life focused on three verbs: **grow, impact and connect.** Every day I try to meet a new person, every week I try to learn something new, every month I try to experience a new adventure and every year I try to make the world better than I did the previous year. Why? Because we have one life and in this one life I want to shake as many hands as I can shake, make as many friends as I can make, see as many sites as my eyes can see and be as many places as my feet can be.

But believe it or not…I wasn't always like this. I wasn't always connecturous and adventurous < *and yes I made up my own word and it means willingness to connect* >. No. I wasn't always adventurous and connecturous, but life taught me to be this way. Life taught me to eff a lot of FEAR and eat a lot of PIE. Not blueberry or apple pie but PIE with a capital P.I.E. It stands for performance, image and exposure and is known to many as the three keys to success. Harvey Coleman introduced this idea and concept in his 1996 best-seller *Empowering Yourself.*

In 1996 he claimed that performance accounts for 10% of our success, image accounts for 20% and exposure accounts for 70%. I wasn't old enough to have an opinion one way or the other, but I was old enough to know that the image of my name preconceived me and it hurt my success more than helped me.

Or so I thought.

As a child, I remember many teachers calling me Lake Eisha even when knowing the correct pronunciation of my name. Unfortunately, the disrespect didn't stop in grade school. It continued into adulthood too.

At 22 I started my first job at Cintas Corporation—you know, the uniform people with the white, blue and red trucks. I was a sales rep trainee and there was a ton of training. A ton for two weeks. Two whole weeks. Maybe even three, but I can't remember correctly. But I do remember my first and most eventful training and that was my day with the Cintas truck drivers.

I remember that day like yesterday.

I was energized, I was excited and I was anxious to prove myself to the world. *The world Craig.* Shout-out to Day-Day from *Friday After Next.* On top of energy, excitement and anxiety—I was also bright-eyed, bushy-tailed and ready to be trained well.

Epic fail.

I walked up to my trainer's truck, opened the heavy metal door, planted my feet on the cold, metal floor and took a seat. She looked at me, I looked at her, she looked at me, I looked at her and then I smiled. I smiled a worthwhile smile and did what most people would do—I introduced myself. "Hi, my name is Keisha and I'm looking forward to riding with you."

Becky didn't say a word. She just looked at me and stared. She sat there in silence and stared at me. With her round face, stringy blonde hair and metal-framed glasses she stared. She stared so long that I felt like I was in elementary school playing the staring game. You know the one < *insert long stare here* >. Then she finally broke her silence, *"Keisha? With that name I'm guessing you're on welfare with multiple kids, right?"*

Wait What.

< insert emoji with big eyes here, insert Kevin Hart's serious face here and Bernie Mac's side-eye >

I just stared. No blinks. Just stares. Like I was in elementary school playing the staring game. No blinks. Just stares. A shocked stare. My eyes remained bright but my tail turned mushy. I literally felt myself sinking into the seat, contemplating if I should cuss Becky out or get out the truck.

Hearing welfare and kids infuriated me, frustrated me and irritated the hell out of me. But more than my many, many thoughts of anger and annoyance—it discouraged me. I wasn't discouraged because it was true—I was discouraged because it COULD have been true.

My grand-momma and poppa were rolling stones. Wherever he laid his hat and wherever she laid her lace handkerchief were their homes. My family's generational curse COULD have made the stereotypes of my name my reality and that discouraged me.

First thought. CUSS BECKY OUT mean girl style with mean girl words. Every one you can think of. Every single one. Very immature thinking on my end—yes. But forget sticks and stones breaking my bones. This lady's words WERE hurting me and I wanted to hurt her back.

Second thought. *Cussing her out will only perpetuate her stereotype and getting out the truck would make me a coward. I am neither.*

Third thought. *What would Jesus do and what would Mom do?* I think they would put on their big girl panties and stand up to Becky. And that's exactly what I did. I looked Becky in her eyes, her metal-framed brown eyes, and mustered one word—WHY.

She sat in silence and looked at me with confusion. It was unexpected confusion, unforeseen confusion and unwavering confusion. But in true Keisha fashion I ignored Becky's confusion and I, a very discouraged, disheartened Keisha, looked Becky back in her eyes and asked why louder, *"Why do you feel this way?"*

I didn't want to approve or disprove her beliefs. After five minutes of silence I just wanted to know WHY. Why she felt the way she did and why she felt the need to say it out loud.

Becky continued to look at me confused and started to stutter Porky Pig-style. It was clear that she was un-clear. Unclear why she felt this way and unclear if she truly felt this way.

Her Porky Pig stuttering continued. But before I could respond or ask her to expound, we pulled up to our first delivery, then our second delivery and then our third. For three hours Becky hid behind uniforms, mops and mats—always finding a way to meticulously place each item in front of her face to block her mouth.

She wasn't ready to answer my question and neither was I ready to hear it. But ready or not, I had to hear it. Ready or not, I needed to hear it. And ready or not, here I come.

Lunch came and Becky couldn't dodge me anymore. There weren't any uniforms, mops or mats preventing us from talking. It was me and her, sitting at a booth in the middle of nowhere Kentucky, eating lunch at the town's favorite 5-star restaurant—Subway.

Becky started talking as soon as we sat down and didn't stop until lunch was over. She spoke of her very limited exposure to black women and black people. She spoke of the news and how the media portrayed "the blacks." She spoke of her upbringing and the stories her family shared, and then she said something she probably didn't mean to say—unlike the welfare comment from earlier—she spoke of her trailer park past and her childhood desire to marry a man that would save her.

Yes. Becky needed to be saved in more ways than one. Society's stereotypes fueled her prejudice. Her prejudice fueled her beliefs and her beliefs fueled her actions. In all truthfulness, she was doing to me what others had done to her. She was prejudging the name Keisha like people prejudged the name Becky and like people prejudged trailer parks. Her past was dark and it influenced her remarks.

At 22, Becky prejudged me based on a name and at 22, I had a choice to make—do I live or run from Keisha?

After the incident with Becky, I grew very embarrassed and ashamed of my name and even thought about changing it. I wasn't giving the name an identity, the name was giving me an identity and this caused me to suffer from an identity crisis. For months I struggled to find myself, and while trying to re-find me, I came across a quote that read:

"Life is not about finding yourself—life is about creating yourself"
GEORGE BERNARD SHAW

That's it, I thought. I will create myself. Kind of like Build-A-Bear but Build-A-Me, and the journey to Build-A-Keisha began.

Step 1: Change my name.

My mom was really upset about the name change idea because she named me Keisha for a reason. I sympathized with her but wanted her to sympathize with me. Heck, she disliked her name too. But in all actuality I didn't dislike my name per say—I disliked the stereotypes people associated with it, so I wanted to change it. I wanted to change it to avoid thoughts and comments like Becky's, and I felt it was easier to change my name than it was to change thoughts and comments like Becky's toward my name. I researched name-changing in Kentucky and was quite surprised by the results. The search revealed that changing your name was quite easy. An adult could simply begin using a new name as long as she/he wasn't trying to get away from creditors or criminal problems. Double check. I wasn't running from either, so the name change idea was becoming more and more promising.

However, in all honesty, I was running from myself and I was hurting my mother in the process. My mom felt responsible for the way I felt, considering she named me, BUT she named me Keisha for a reason. She was hurt because I was hurt, and as she always says, *"You will never truly understand or know this feeling until you have kids of your own one day."* I didn't know that feeling, but I did know the feeling of thoughts like Becky's.

But Mom named me Keisha for a reason.

I was born two months premature. I was 3 pounds and 14 ounces and I could fit in the palm of an adult's hand. My birth was indeed a blessing, so for that reason Mom named me Keisha, meaning *"favorite daughter."*

But favorite daughter doesn't typically pop into the minds of folks when hearing Keisha or any other isha. Society doesn't paint this picture, the media doesn't paint this picture and neither does the great philosopher Lil Wayne's 1999 song *Kisha* nor does the 2012 summer hit *Cashin' Out*—better known as *Smoking on that Keisha.*

Both songs paint Keisha as a promiscuous woman treated more like property than a person and Keisha the drug people smoke to get intoxicated. None paint Keisha as a favorite daughter, so at 22 I was stuck between a rock and a hard place. At 22 I didn't want to hurt Mom's feelings, but I disliked the image people associated with Keisha. I disliked images like Becky's, but Mom's image trumped Becky's image and the journey continued.

Step 2: Redefine Keisha's image.

I texted 50+ friends and asked the following question— who am I? Definitely a loaded question to get via text! My friends were confused to say THE LEAST (I tend to have that effect on people these days) but they played along.

You are a:

* *Natural Connector*

* *Creative Visionary*

* *Strategic Leader*

* *Resourceful Researcher*

* *Analytical Problem-Solver*

* *Purposeful Planner*

* *Teacher, Facilitator and Trainer*

* *Future Executive, CEO and Entrepreneur*

Not sure what I would have done if I would've gotten things like *you are a spoiled brat*. I mean it's kind of true, being the baby of four brothers and all, but who wants to hear that? Lucky for me, my friends told me exactly what I needed to hear and I rewrote Keisha's image with the help of their words. And in that moment I stopped running from the thing I needed to run to—myself.

But the running didn't stop there. I also ran to a MBA, I ran to boards and I ran to awards. Like parking, I STILL NEEDED VALIDATION. I still needed to guarantee that I wasn't going to become Becky's Keisha, and this made me plague driven not purpose driven.

I was on a path of chasing wall decorations not dreams—struggling to find my identity in a name deemed unprofessional by society. Struggling to find my identity in a name considered to be ghetto and too ethnic. Struggling to find my identity in a name associated with welfare and multiple kids. Struggling.

Society didn't want me to be Keisha and neither did Becky. Society wanted me to be Ke$ha—with or without the dollar sign—and people treated me as such. We wear our names like we wear our clothes, so people treated me one way when they thought my name was Ke$ha and another way after learning my name was Keisha. It was infuriating, frustrating, irritating, annoying and most of all discouraging. At 25 I was experiencing the same feelings I felt at 22 when I rode with Becky. At 25, I was back in that Cintas truck.

On September 27, 2009, I wrote:

> *Life is a resume builder. We spend our whole lives looking for ways to build our resume. Are we building our resume for ourselves or are we building our resume to impress people? If our resume wasn't visible to the world, would we work ourselves to death trying to build our education, experience, community involvement and skillset as America sees fit? Would we try so hard to reach the American Dream or would we recreate our own? When did the American Dream become everyone's dream?*

I wrote these words not knowing if I should shoot for Ke$ha's Dream or Keisha's Dream. I wrote these words not knowing why society wanted me to be Ke$ha not Keisha. I wrote these words. I was Keisha and Mom named me Keisha for a reason.

I was 25 and lost.

I was 25 experiencing a quarter-life crisis.

I was 25 melting down.

So what now? After much praying and much journaling, I thought back to George Bernard Shaw's quote, *"Life is not about finding yourself—life is about creating yourself."* I was Keisha and she was me and I could create Keisha to be whatever she wanted to be. Screw Becky and screw society. Keisha was my name and that name was here to stay.

Step 3: Live Keisha's dream and that's exactly what I did!

In order to live Keisha's dream, I knew I needed mentorship and guidance. I knew because no one gets anywhere alone. An old parable taught me that *it takes a village to raise a child* and life taught me that *it takes mentors, advocates and sponsors to continue raising adults.* So I sought after mentors. And not just one but 20.

I contacted my local Chamber of Commerce and introduced myself. Then I told them what I was seeking. I told them that I was a recent college graduate trying to forge my path. I told them that I was interested in business and education and wanted to find a way to combine the two. I told them that I was looking for mentorship and guidance. I told them that I wanted to meet with 20 leaders in my community doing things of interest to me. And lastly, I asked them to recommend folks for me to meet and to introduce me.

They did more than that!

They gave me a scholarship to the *Greater Louisville Idea Development Expedition*—a two-day conference designed to connect and engage Louisville's current generation and next generation of community leaders. Talk about a perfect fit! And I was one of only four chosen to receive the scholarship.

For two days I connected and engaged with more than 100 community leaders from the mayor of the city to councilwomen, councilmen, CEOS, VPS and everything in between. It was life changing to say the least.

Following the conference, I spent the next 100 days reconnecting with the councilwomen, councilmen, CEOS and VPS from the retreat. I met with one person daily over coffee or tea to learn about life, leadership and happiness from their unique perspective. I listened intensively, took extensive notes and used their guidance to create the Keisha I wanted Keisha to be.

A Keisha that wanted to help people realize their full potential. A Keisha that wanted to mentor, educate and inspire. A Keisha that wanted to equip people with the tools they needed to be their best selves. A Keisha that wanted to change the world one connection at a time by connecting people to people and people to resources.

At 25, Harvey Coleman's formula for success finally made sense to me and I was finally old enough to have an opinion one way or the other. My opinion...he was wrong. Success was less about performance and more about exposure, connections and genuine, authentic relationships—yes. But image was way more important than 20%.

The image I had for myself was a key factor to my

success and so was the image others had for me too. But I was the creator of my image and I had to realize that. I had to realize that the world didn't define me. I defined me, and then it was my job to tell the world my definition and make the world endorse it. And in that moment of self-actualization and calling Coleman wrong—my love connection with connecting and branding began.

After connecting with the community leaders, I finally had a clear vision of my dream and joined Teach For America. I was placed in St. Louis, Missouri, to teach 8th-grade science and I didn't know a soul but I did have a goal. *Make 100 friends in 100 days* and that's exactly what I did.

At 28, I completed my two-year teaching commitment with Teach For America and started a new job with a new company. With the new role came a new goal. *Meet 100 co-workers in 100 days* and I met more than 200.

At 30, I got my dream job launching a social innovation startup. Startups require market validations and market validations require connections. You guessed it. I connected with 100+ people in 100 days. And then at 32 I started my own agency and I did the same thing. I connected with 100 more people in 100 days.

In the pages that follow I will share 100 ways to connect with 100 people in 100 days. I have used them all, all 100 of them except three, over the course of 10 years. Each way has helped me push my performance, influence my image and expand my exposure. Each way has helped me feel zen, get in, earn wins and make friends. And each way has made my transitions better and easier to weather.

So I ask of you.

MY STORY Are you transitioning? Meaning. Are you of the transitioning kind? Are you graduating or relocating? Are you job hunting or promotion wanting? Are you empty nesting or manifesting? Whether one, two or a combination of a few—this book is for you!

Let your connection journey begin.

Part One: Prep

Before you can connect there's a few things you should do to prep. Connection success is where connection preparation meets connection opportunities so I highly advise, recommend and suggest that you prep before you connect.

*Shout-out to Zig Ziglar and the rest that claim the original version of this quote.

Set A Goal

I don't know about you but I need goals. And not just any goals but smart goals. Super-smart goals. The timeliness of smart goals holds me accountable and the measurability of them motivates me.

If you tell me to do push-ups for 60 seconds I am going to do as few as possible. Why? Because I have the upper-body strength of a two-year-old. But if you tell me to do 20 push-ups in 60 seconds I am going to ignore the two-year-old living in my arms and complete the 20 push-ups by any means necessary. Any means!!!

The same holds true for connecting. You need a goal and not just any goal. You need a smart goal. The title of this book is a smart goal—*connect with 100 people in 100 days*. This may sound like a lot but it can be done. Just breath, relax and have some fun.

I have connected with 100 people in 100 days several times in my life: when I graduated school, when I started a new role, when I moved to a new state and when I was looking for a new date. Yes a date. We've all been in these shoes a time or two or three so don't judge me friend. Don't judge me.

We've all been here, there and somewhere in between and by here, there and somewhere I mean transitioning. Transitions can be exhilarating and frightening, thrilling and trying, inspiring and mixed with a little bit of crying. But friends and support systems make everything better and connections make transitions easier to weather.

When I was transitioning and connecting I had the same goal every time. Every single time. My goal: connect with 100 people in 100 days. But the ways in which I approached my 100 were always different.

Sometimes I connected with one person a day, other times I connected with two or three people a day. Sometimes I connected with people over coffee, sometimes over lunch and other times over brunch. Sometimes I connected with people at events and other times I connected with people online.

But every single time I connected with 100 people in 100 days. Now it's your turn. You have the goal and you have the approach below—now go.

Note: My definition of connecting is an in-person chat. An in-person chat in which you connect. It can be over coffee, tea, lunch, brunch or at various other things like conferences and events. But the key to connecting is meeting. To meet in person and share your stories.

Personally, I prefer to meet at conferences and events or over coffee and tea since lunch and brunch can get expensive. But if you have the means, by all means, meet over lunch, brunch, dinner or even dunch. Just make sure you meet. Capisce?

PREP 2

Chart Your Connections

You've set a goal. Check. Know what's next? A connection chart. I want you to kick-start your 100 in 100 with a connection chart. A connection chart is a quick and easy way to chart the connections you want to curate and cultivate. These connections can be old, new, borrowed or blue and you can connect with them anywhere and everywhere. On planes. On trains. In lines. And even while you dine. My point. You can connect anywhere and everywhere. Everywhere and anywhere. There's no limit friend.

So what does a connection chart look like? Your connection chart can be a list in a notebook, a table in an Excel spreadsheet or a chart on a whiteboard. You name it…I've used all three!

To start your chart, think about the groups you are involved with or have been involved with over the course of your lifetime. Yes. Your lifetime. Not just adulthood but childhood too. Need help? Associations, organizations, boards, camps, clubs, church, clientele, cohorts, college, colleagues, fellowships, conferences, events, family, fraternities, sororities, friends, hobbies, masterminds, mentors, social media, sports and travel groups to name a few.

Ok. Maybe more than a few. I named more like 20. But the more groups you can generate, the more connections you can make. If we do the math, 100 connections divided by 20 groups equals five connections per group. Only five. You can do this. Piece of cake. Piece of pie.

Next. Write the name of your groups at the top of your list, table or chart and the names of the connections you want to curate and cultivate under each corresponding group. That's it my friend. That is it.

You should also develop a wish list—a wish list of

connections you seek to get. Just write "wish list" at the top of your list and list the topmost connections you wish to meet. In addition to lifetime groups and wish list groups, you can also curate and cultivate other types of connections too, like mentors, advocates and sponsors or groups of peeps that have skillsets you seek.

When I was graduating, my connection chart groups were formed by leadership lessons I wanted to learn and salaries I wanted to earn. When I was relocating, my connection chart groups were based on the associations and organizations I wanted to get plugged into and the social things I wanted to do. When I was job hunting and promotion wanting, my connection chart groups were formed by the jobs and industries I aspired to be in and HR folks I wanted to befriend. And when I was starting and launching my company, my connection chart groups were based on potential stakeholders, partners and supporters.

As you can see, your groups do not have to be limited and you can define them as you wish. The purpose of the chart and the groups is to get you started. To give you a point to start. I repeat. Your connection chart is a start. It's not your end-all/be-all connection plan.

It's a chart to get you started. It's a chart to show you the various avenues and venues you can use to make connections. It's not a chart that should limit your connections by any means. Remember, there's no limit friend and it's totally fine to make connections that are not on your chart. Just add them in as you go.

If you remember my connection journey from the pre-chapter, my connection chart started with a list of

20 community leaders. Well. In theory it did. It really was a list of zero but it grew from 0 to 100 real quick. Real quick. Real quick. Thanks to the Chamber and a shout-out to Drake the rapper.

And now that song is stuck in my head but friend you can do the same. To start your chart, you can chart the initial 20 connections you want to make and fill in the rest as you go. Use the ways below to connect with the initial 20 and then ask the initial 20 that you meet to recommend and introduce you to peeps. Or. You can chart zero connections. You heard me right. I said zero.

You can chart zero connections and use the ways below to meet peeps organically while you're on the go. Or. You can chart the 100 connections you want to make if you're type A and that's a-ok too. Or. You can do a combination of two.

Nonetheless, if you start by charting a few groups, DON'T be so dead set on your groups that you forget to connect with the folks standing or sitting right next to you on planes, on trains, in lines and while you dine! Don't miss out on connection opportunities by being picky. There are great people without great fame and these great people may be staring you dead in your face one day.

GROUP 1	GROUP 2	GROUP 3	GROUP 4	GROUP 5

Chart 1: Sample connection chart template

Share Your Who

Before you can connect with others, YOU (capital Y.O.U.) have to connect with yourself first. WHO ARE YOU? Not what do you do. But who are you? Do you know?

In the pre-chapter I shared my who through my story, BUT that isn't the who I share when connecting and that isn't the who I want you to share when connecting either. That was the long version. The extra-long version. The extended long version. The bonus track. I want you to share the complete opposite. I want you to share a compact connection who. A condensed version. An extra-short version. The non-bonus track.

My connection who sounds like this:

> *"Hello, my name is Keisha Mabry and I help people build genuine, authentic relationships to realize their dreams."*

Or.

> *"Hello, my name is Keisha Mabry. I help transitionals find their 'IT' and get connected to it in 100 days."*

Or.

> *"Hello, my name is Keisha Mabry and I am most passionate about connecting people to people and people to resources."*

Versus my networking do:

> *"Hello, my name is Keisha Mabry and I am the founder and CEO of The Connection Curator."*

See the difference?

Both can be said in approximately the same amount of time, but the who gives more insight into me while the do gives more insight into my company. You may be wondering why I have three who statements. Yep I do, and I share whichever who makes sense for the audience I am connecting with.

Make sense?

Probably not. I'm sure you're wondering what this who-sharing looks like in practice, so I'm glad you asked. But even if you didn't, here's a hint and a blueprint.

In the beginning it can be hard to share your who, hard to share your story not your glory and hard to focus on the person not the profession. Hard because first you have to break your do habit. And second you have to break everyone else's do habit too.

We live in a world of networkers used to doing networkey things like shoving business cards in our faces without saying anything. Or. Talking our heads off about their titles and their glories. Or. Freezing up when they hear the *what's your story* question. So moving from the profession to the person, from the glory to the story and from the do to the who can be hard at first but not impossible.

When meeting someone for the first time at a conference or event. My mind works like this. I approach or they approach and we shake hands, say hellos and swap names. If they speak first, they, 99% of the time, will tell me their employer, their title and that's it. Then they will ask me *what do you do*. What do I do? Deep

sigh. Why must we exchange dos before whos?
Any who.

Instantly my stomach turns, churns and burns, and
instead of sharing my do I share my who in return. I
say, *"I help people build genuine, authentic relationships to
realize their dreams."* Or. *"I help transitionals find their
'IT' and get connected to it in 100 days."* Or. *"I am most
passionate about connecting people to people and people to
resources."* Then I say, *"I know you told me what you do but
what's your story? Who are you?"*

And from there they share. They share their who, using
my who as an example, and then they ask me follow-up
questions like, *what's a transitional, how do you build
relationships and how did you become interested in connecting?* I answer and ask them follow-up questions about
their who too, and just like that we connect. But if I
speak first everything gets reversed. I will share my
name, my who and then I will say, *"What's your story?"*
Get it? Got it? Good!

When meeting someone for this first time over coffee
or tea, especially if I called the meeting, I thank them
for seeing me and then I usually start the conversation
by saying *what's your story* as a way to get the conversation started. And like a charm it works every time but
this time there's no script. This time the person can say
whatever comes to mind and it's usually a combination
of a who and a do. And that's fine too as long as you
two end up sharing your whos.

Just keep in mind that connecting is relational not
transactional, so connecting should be more about you
and less about your company, more about your person

and less about your profession, more about your passions and purpose and less about the title of the 9-to-5 you work just to stay alive. So if you still haven't picked up what I'm putting down—I want you to share your connection who, not your networking do.

Use the exercise below to write the words to your who. Don't worry about the sentence itself just yet. Right now I just want you to focus on getting words that resonate with you on paper. I want you to brainstorm and brain-dump now and wordsmith later. I mean it friend. Wordsmith later. No perfectionism in the interim. You can craft and perfect your sentence later. Now follow my directions and get connecting.

DIRECTIONS

1. Collect any and all professional development self-assessments you have ever taken in life, or, as many as you can locate. If you have never taken any assessments, you should try these on for size.

    Examples of self-assessments can include, but are not limited to: 360s, Cognitive Process Profile, Emergenetics, Herrmann Brain Dominance Instrument, Life Entrepreneurship, LinkedIn Endorsements, Myers-Briggs and StrengthsFinder as well as input from family, friends and mentors.

2. Print hard copies of the results.

3. Highlight every adjective and noun used to describe you.

4. Look for trends and write the top two to three adjectives and the top two to three nouns in the corresponding boxes below.

5. Fill in the rest of the boxes with three whos, three whats and PREP three whys.

6. Combine all five pieces of the activity and voilà, a who statement.

7. Write three different who statements using the space below the boxes.

   Example language can be:

   EXAMPLE 1
   I am a _____ that helps_____ to_____.

   EXAMPLE 2
   I help _____ do_____ to_____.

   EXAMPLE 3
   I am most passionate about _____.

8. Read each who statement out loud and pick the statement(s) that appeal most to you.

9. Wordsmith. Now you can wordsmith. Wordsmith your chosen statement(s) by adding words, replacing words and removing words until it flows naturally.

   Start sharing your who until it feels comfortable to you.

ADJECTIVES adjectives used to describe you	NOUNS nouns used to describe you
example: passionate, energetic	*example: connector, coach*
WHO who you spend the majority of your time helping / serving	WHAT what you are doing to help / serve your who
example: transitionals	*example: find their IT*
WHY what motivates you to help / serve your who (the why)	
example: build genuine, authentic relationships and get connected to *their IT in 100 days*	

Chart 2: Who statement template

WHO STATEMENT 1

_____

_____ P R E P

_____

_____

WHO STATEMENT 2

_____

_____

_____

_____

WHO STATEMENT 3

_____

_____

_____

_____

JUST IN CASE YOU MESS UP THE FIRST TIME

WHO STATEMENT I

_____

_____

_____

_____

WHO STATEMENT 2

_____

_____

_____

_____

WHO STATEMENT 3

_____

_____

_____

_____

Say Yes

Friend. You have a connection goal. You have a connection chart. You have a who statement. Now you just need to start. Now you just need to say yes. Not to the dress but to new connects. I mean say yes to the dress too if it's the dress for you but that's not the yes I am currently referring to. I am referring to your connection yes.

In her 2015 book, *Year of Yes*, Shonda Rhimes talks about a transformational year in which she said yes to all of the offers that came her way. She said yes even when fear said no. Saying yes transformed her life and it can transform yours too.

Connecting with people can be a scary thing for introverts, an overwhelming thing for busy folks and an unexciting thing for those that subscribe to the "no new friends" motto. Scary, overwhelming and unexciting. Not the things we typically say yes to but I want you to. I want you to say yes to all three because there's value in connecting.

I say yes to all three daily even when I don't want to say yes. I'm an extrovert but sometimes I get scared, sometimes I get busy, sometimes I get overwhelmed and sometimes I get sleepy. And when feeling these, I don't want to connect, I want to rest. I want to lie in my bed with Netflix and chill.

But then I remember my motto—new **You**, new **Goal**, new **Grad**, new **Role**, new **Startup**, new **State**, new **Career**, new **Mate**? Connect with 100 people in 100 days to feel Zen, get In, earn Wins and make Friends!—I remember my motto and I say yes. I remember my motto and I connect. I say no to Netflix and I say yes to connect.

Well sometimes I say yes to both because Netflix is therapeutic for me and self-care is key. So in other words, I find a way to do both. I'll schedule connection time before 9, work time between 9 and 5 and Netflix time after 5. Or. I'll schedule connection time during the week and Netflix time on the weekend.
You get it friend?

Part Two: Live

Many people avoid building relationships and I kind of understand why. They think it's too time consuming or they are overwhelmingly shy. And it's true. It's a commitment that takes courage and persistence BUT it's extremely significant. And for the record, you can connect by simply being you. By simply living how you normally live and doing what you normally do. So live.

Say Hello

A simple hello can lead to a million things. A million things! But we pass people on a daily basis without saying anything. Nothing. Not one thing. We pass people on a daily basis without saying a simple hello. On planes. On trains. In lines. And while we dine. We say nothing but we should. We should say something. We should say hello.

When transitionals come to me for connection coaching, we always start here. We always start with hello. Whether introverted or extroverted, we always start at hello because all connections start with hello, because hello can lead to a million things and because once people master hello they can master connecting.

Want to see? I know seeing is believing so keep on reading.

One transitional client of mine was a transplant living in a new state where she knew no one and I do mean no one. No one friend. She said hello to a stranger while in line at a coffee shop and was immediately taken under the stranger's wings.

The stranger happened to be a well-connected local that introduced the transplant to many new friends. The transplant's many new friends helped her get into many new circles and feel a sense of less loneliness and more zen. And just like that a simple hello led to new friends.

Another transitional client of mine was a lifestyle and

entertainment guru with a new goal. He was trying to
expand his brand into new markets, so I encouraged
him to say hello to everyone he encountered. Everyone
and everywhere. Everywhere and everyone. On planes,
on trains, in lines and while he dined.

One day while on a plane he said hello to the passenger
sitting next to him who happened to be a lifestyle and
entertainment guru too. The two talked the entire
plane ride about different ways they could expand
worldwide. And just like that a simple hello led to the
accomplishment of a new goal.

Other transitional clients have acquired new clients by
saying hello, new jobs by saying hello, new dates and
new mates by saying hello. Hello is a simple word with
five letters but hello can lead to a million things, thangs
and everything in between from new goals to new
beaus, so start saying hello. **Side note:** Sometimes
people won't say hello back and that's okay just keep
saying it anyway.

2.2

Listen

How well do you listen? Not how well do you hear but
how well do you listen? Especially when asking that
dreaded question *how's your day going*. Many of us ask it
out of habit not really wanting a response. Many of us
ask it out of habit not really wanting to listen. But I
encourage you to change your tactic and listen if only
for a minute.

Personally, I enjoy asking this dreaded question because it's not so dreaded to me. Instead it's a connection opportunity and I ask it daily. I ask cashiers, peers, baristas and fashionistas, bank tellers, elders, waitresses and acquaintances. I ask it and I listen.

I listen to the nodders that just nod and say, *"Going well."* I listen to the thankers that thank me for asking and then ask me the question in return. I listen to the happy campers that respond with words like *"absolutely amazing"* while smiling from ear to ear and cheek to cheek. I listen to the ready-to-get-off-workers that tell me the time they get off, the time they got in and the hours they've put in. I listen to the optimists that say things like, *"Not too bad. I've had worse."* I listen to the pessimists that say things like, *"Meh. I've had better."* And last but not least I listen to the venters.

For many, the venters are like splinters—annoying pains to avoid. But for me, the venters are people that just need a listening ear. So I listen. I listen and chat, and by listening I make a new connect.

2.3

Be Happy

According to the laws of attraction, connectivity and relativity, we attract the energy we put into the universe. Positive energy attracts positive energy and negative energy attracts negative energy. Think about it. We all have a friend, colleague or family member with an upbeat, positive personality and like bees to honey, positivity flocks to this person but negativity flees. On the contrary, we all have a friend, colleague or family member with a downbeat, negative personality and like flies to vinegar, positivity flees from this person but negativity flocks.

Are you honey or are you vinegar? Honey I hope. Because as Nanna would say, you can catch more bees and flies with honey than you can with vinegar. And in the connection world, you can catch more connections with happiness than you can with sadness.

People prefer to connect with those who are positive and happy and Nanna would agree. Like positivity, happiness is like honey to bees and people are naturally attracted to these types of peeps. Think back to the friend, colleague and family members above. Would you rather connect with the upbeat, positive and happy peeps or the downbeat, negative and sad peeps? I vote for the happy and positive peeps. I vote for honey.

So again I ask. Are you honey or vinegar? When we are honey, we exude happiness and positivity, we look approachable and, like magnets, we attract. When we are honey, we show the world our smile, the world smiles back and, like magic, we connect.

2.4

Smize

Earlier I made a generalization. An assumption. A statement. I said, *when we are happy we show the world our smile.* But this isn't always the case. I'm a happy person and I always have resting bitch face. I have resting bitch face even when I think I'm smiling.

What is resting bitch face? Just google Kanye.

Resting bitch face says everything but hey friend hey. Resting bitch face says go away and have a nice day. To mitigate my resting bitch face I smirk and smize. Smize means to smile with your eyes, so I smirk with my lips and smize with my eyes. But believe you me, this is not easy-peasy. As stated earlier, I have resting bitch face even when I think I'm smiling!

I have yet to perfect my smize but am well on my way and to practice my smize I take a selfie a day. That's right friend. A selfie a day because resting bitch face keeps connections away. So what does your face say? Does it say hey friend hey or go away and have a nice day?

P.S. If you want more practice perfecting this way all you have to do is look up Tyra Banks.

2.5

Don't Smize

I know I just told you to smize but sometimes the opposite works well too. Sometimes the opposite works even better. When I forget to smize, people stare at me, they stop me on the street and they say things to me. They say things like *you're too pretty not to smile* or *I hope your day gets better*. It's a bit blunt yes but it definitely makes for an interesting way to connect.

2.6

Complement Continuously

They say imitation is the best form of flattery. Well. I
say flattery is the best form of friendship-making.
When I see and meet people, I become an instant spy.
A secret agent. A detective. I become observant. I do a
quick once-over without being noticed and take mental
notes of unique jewelry, tattoos and clothing—any and
everything that can help me spark a conversation. I
learned this skill in sales and I must say I do it pretty
damn well.

I'm so good that I've even mastered the look-but-don't-
look methodology. You know the one. You're out with
family or friends and they say look at xyz, you turn to
look and then they say don't look. You sit confused for
a bit but then you realize they want you to look-but-
don't-look or in other words they want you to look
discreetly.

But back to the complimenting. After the mental note,
the next step is flattery. *"Nice watch,"* I'll say. Or. *"Cool
tattoo."* Then I wait. I wait for the story. There's always
a story. Stories about bowties and music note tattoos,
vintage skirts and cool shoes. Stories. Sparked by
compliments. Stories. That lead to connections.

2.7

Be Cool

People like to be connected to two things: cool ish and
cool peeps. Peeps that go places people want to go, do

things people want to do, see things people want to see, meet peeps people want to meet and say ish people want to say but can't. Now granted. Cool is subjective.

Cool can mean different things to different peeps and cool can range drastically from hairstyles to lifestyles to textiles to something else worthwhile. But one thing always remains consistent with cool and that is truth. Yes friend. Cool is truth.

Cool means being true to you. It means being authentic. It means being genuine. Being cool means you do what you do without the permission of others. It means you are uniquely you and unapologetically you. It means you are one speed with no pleasing, and people flock to this type of coolness. People flock to this type of youness because when you are you—you give other people permission to be them. When you are you—people are attracted to you because being you has superpowers.

However, many never tap into these superpowers. Many never tap into their superhuman features and abilities because instead they are too focused on pleasing. They live double lives. They are one way with their friends, another way with their family, one way with their mentors and another way with their colleagues. They are in essence lip syncers, and eventually they are going to miss a beat and someone is going to call them out on their inability to lip sync.

And that my friend is why it pays to be one speed. That my friend is why it pays to be you. That my friend is why it pays to be cool. To be your cool, authentic and genuine self unapologetically. By being cool you will attract the peeps you're supposed to attract and repel the peeps you're not. That's the sign of a good brand, so be yourself because other selfs are taken my friend.

2.8

Have Swag

Have you ever noticed someone as soon as they walk in the room? Like as soon as they walk in the room their presence is made known? You can't quite put your finger on it but you, like many others, want to know who they are? Well. That my friend is swag and you need to get you some. And not to brag but I have swag.

<insert girl emoji with hair flip here>

So what exactly is swag? This is debatable but to me swag is a combination of three things: clothing, confidence and charisma or charm. But the most important question is how can you get you some?

I believe it starts with clothing. Then clothing leads to confidence and confidence leads to charisma and charm. I am sure many psychologists, psychiatrists and counselors will disagree with me but this is my truth and I speak nothing but my truth. I do agree that one must build confidence inside out, but there's something about one's outer appearance that makes them feel confident. Years of watching Maury's makeovers taught me this and so did years of teaching adolescents.

There's just something about feeling good when you look good, and clothes help with that. When I look good I feel good and when I look good I chat more. I chat more because clothing opens the door to conversation, and when I dress my best, I feel confident. When I dress my best, I get compliments and the compliments always lead to conversation.

So yes. I'm telling you to dress. I'm telling you to dress your best. I'm telling you to dress for success and I'm telling you to dress to connect. BUT I'm not telling you to go spend a ton of money on clothes and I'm not telling you to adhere to crazy, unrealistic standards of beauty. I'm just telling you that there's confidence in clothing—hence the term power suit.

Side note: Who still wears suits? I don't think I even own one these days. I have power shoes not power suits. Any who. I want you to find your power suit, shoe, shirt or tie, turn your swag on and become a social butterfly. Now fly friend fly.

2.9

Wear Tees

There are plenty of graphic tees. Tees from colleges, tees from clubs, tees from sports teams and tees that say free hugs. Graphic tees turn you into a walking billboard because the shirt speaks first. The shirt speaks without you having to say anything. Well eventually. Eventually you have to say something, but in the beginning the shirt speaks.

Like shirts, buttons speak too. I wear a button daily—well almost daily—that says *"hey friend."* Some days I forget I'm wearing it and then I hear strangers say *"hey friend"* on planes, on trains, in lines and while I dine. I say *"hey friend"* back and just like that we start to chat. So find a tee, find a button and start your day with some social shoulder-rubbing.

2.10

Be Kitschy

To many, kitschy means tacky, but to me it means connection cheesiness. It's a cheesy and easy thing one already does or can do to spark conversation. You've seen it. I know you have—the guy that always wears the bubble vest, the lady that always wears a brooch on her chest, the guy that wears cool kicks and bowties and the lady that wears pink glasses on her eyes. You've seen it and you've thought about it. You've seen it and you've wanted to know the story behind it. You've seen it and you've asked about it.

Do you have a thing? A kitschy thing? It can be how you wear your hair or how you wear your clothes. It can be colorful socks or a piercing in your nose. It can be anything—even slang. It can be anything—even deranged. My thing is part slang and part deranged. I'm known for my "hey friend" salutation and my vintage jewelry fixation. And when I say fixation, I mean fixation. I love thrifting and I thrift frequently. Really frequently, and all of my thrifted pieces are kitschy and they make starting conversations easy-peasy.

I also wear a lot of black and white but this hasn't become my thing just yet. I don't wear it consistently enough, so Janelle Monáe still has that trend in the bag. And that's the thing about this way. Your thing. Your kitschy thing has to be a consistent thing and it also has to be a noticeable thing. Something that people can see easily and something that has meaning.

The key is to have a story behind it. A story that people can relate to. A story that people can connect with you through, and a story that rings true to you. So before you go all willy-nilly with kitschy, think about things you already wear, do or say that can spark conversation with the people that pass your way. Get it? Got it? Good! Go forth and conquer kitschyhood.

2.11

Ambassador a Brand

Brand ambassadors have a portfolio of products they represent, and their goal is to get others to try them. Some brand ambassadors have only one product in their portfolio while others have a few. You probably have seen them in your city. They give away food samples at the grocery store and liquor samples at the bar. They wear certain clothes and drive certain cars.

These brand ambassador roles are typically paid but some are not. Some peeps ambassador brands just to get stuff for cheap or stuff for free. I'm a brand ambassador for a jewelry company that I adore. It's unpaid, but I get wholesale discounts on chokers and most importantly I get exposure.

But—there's always a but—these roles can be hard to come by. Sometimes you have to apply and other times you are scouted. Nevertheless, it's a really cool way to connect because you can affect the lifecycle of a brand while getting new followers and new friends.

2.12

Make a Purchase

Sometimes connections come with a price, and not the price you're probably thinking of. So what the heck am I talking about? I'm talking about the price you pay when you're purchasing things. Huh? Yes purchasing. Purchasing provides a perfect opportunity to connect. We purchase things on a daily basis without taking advantage of these great opportunities to spark conversations and make connections.

Think about it.

You probably purchase at least one thing daily, or at the very least weekly, and while purchasing your one thing, you can make a new friend. I have made many friends while making purchases. My eyebrow lady, my makeup lady, my beautician, my barista, the bartender at my favorite bar, the guy that works on my car—all of these friendships started with a purchase. So purchase until your money ends and make some new friends. But STAY WITHIN YOUR BUDGET FRIEND. Stay within your budget.

2.13

Read Nametags

Whether or not we want to admit it—we have all heard voices. We have all heard someone call our name, only to turn around and see no one there. Or maybe there was someone there in your case. Any who. We have all been there.

Hearing our name causes an immediate response. An immediate reaction. An immediate neck turn. We instantly turn our attention to the voice in question and pay attention. And for this very reason, I Read Nametags.

I read nametags to address strangers by their names and instantly there's a flame. Instantly it feels like we've known each other for years. Now granted. People don't just walk around wearing nametags, so this way works only in certain circumstances. But it works, so if you don't buy it—try it.

My favorite way to use this way is at events and when making purchases, and it's so worth it. I connect with the person serving me or ringing me up and every time, every single time, this way works like the drop of a dime. Sometimes I get free stuff like free food and free drinks, but all of the times I meet new peeps.

2.14

Eat Your Dinner

My two favorite hobbies are eating and deciding what to eat next. Food really is one of my best friends, and if I could list eating on my resume—I would!

I eat a lot. A whole lot. But I don't eat a lot of big meals. I eat a lot of small meals, which creates a lot of small windows of connection opportunities.

And when I eat I always try to think about folks that can eat with me. Whether it's a morning coffee and pastry or an afternoon brunch, a late lunch or an early dunch. Oh. Dunch is the meal after lunch but before dinner—I told you I eat a lot.

I eat a lot out and I eat a lot in, so there's always an opening to eat with a friend. Friends eat with me on Saturdays when I grocery shop, on Sundays when I meal prep and during the week when I restaurant hop. Did I mention I eat a lot? I do, and I don't know why the food I pack daily is never good enough to eat when it's time to take my lunch break. I always want something else no matter what I make, so I spend most of my lunch breaks in fast food casual lines.

Please don't judge the way I spend my time. There's a lesson in my food obsession. The lesson is the title to Keith Ferrazzi's book *Never Eat Alone*. He was right. You should never eat alone. You gotta eat and you should use eating as a window of connection opportunity.

There's more than one way to cook an egg and there's more than one way to connect over food. You can simply do what I do and invite folks to have lunch with you. Or. You can invite folks to run food errands with you, like farmers market shopping. Or. You can invite folks to a friends' night out of food truck hopping, pop-up restaurants, progressive dinners or food swapping. You can even join, lead or create a food club, befriend some chefs or do all of the above.

Me personally. My all-time favorite food connections have happened at food clubs I joined, created or led.

And I've led a few, but I started my first food club when I moved to St. Lou.

I started a lunch club at work as a quick and easy way to meet my colleagues. The name of the lunch club was Global Gourmet and it brought 8-10 people together on a bimonthly basis to experience different types of cuisine in new places. We ate Thai, Japanese, French, Mexican, Chinese, Mediterranean, Indian and Cajun. We ate to our heart's content, and from the experience we grew closer as friends.

When I left the company, the lunch club continued and I'm excited to say that three years later it still exists today. I still go back from time to time to eat with old colleagues and their new counterparts. Some of the peeps have changed, but the goal has stayed the same— to connect with colleagues over food—and you can do this too.

My second-all-time favorite food connections have happened at brunch. I'm not sure if it's the bottomless mimosas or my love for breakfast food, but I could eat brunch for every meal of the day. Every single meal. In fact, I'm craving brunch as we speak. Or as I type I should say. And I'm not the only one that loves brunch. Saturday and Sunday brunch has become a thing. Like a real thing that people do. And sometimes venues require reservations too!

Speaking of brunch. A few of my friends have even started a brunch-run club called bRUNch. They get up early on Saturday morning, run and exercise for an hour or two and then meet up at a nearby restaurant for brunch. My mind loves the idea, but my heart does not. My mind says go run, but my heart says get more sleep. If I listened to my mind, I could lose a few pounds and meet more peeps. But with or without the run—brunch is a treat. You can get good eats and you can meet good peeps.

But again, there's more than one way to cook an egg and there's more than one way to connect over food. You can use some of the ways I use—if you choose—or create your own. You can meet up with friends out or at home. Ain't nothing to it but to do it, so just—do it.

2.15
Sample Samples

When I was little, my mother would take my brother and me to sample samples on Saturdays. We would sample samples at the grocery store and Sam's Club, at Costco and the mall. We would run our errands and sample samples all over the city trying new foods while meeting new friendlies.

I'm no longer little in age but I'm little in heart and I still sample samples on Saturdays while pushing my cart. I sample at Trader Joe's, Cost Plus World Market, Total Wine, food courts and more. I sample everything I pass on my way in and out the door. While sampling, I always eat new treats and meet new peeps but the more I try the more I buy.

< insert a deep sigh and a cry here >

Do Chores

We all have stuff that needs to get done and a lot of this stuff isn't a whole lot of fun. From laundry to cleaning, shopping to painting, moving to hanging, lifting to shifting, delivery to assembly and everything in between. We all have stuff. A whole lot of, whole lot of, whole lot of stuff sitting on to-do lists and honey-do lists waiting on us to get to it.

And all this stuff takes all this time BUT have you ever combined your stuff with a friend and some wine? I do it all the time! **Side note:** I'm not a beer drinker but I could imagine stuff being paired with a friend and a beer or two, or maybe three or as many as you need.

Think about it.

We all have stuff to do. So why not get it done in twos, threes or even fours? Why not connect with folks while doing your chores? It's the best! And you can get your stuff done faster too, providing more time to do other things you really want to do like sleep, read or watch reality TV. Sounds like winning to me.

P.S. You can also connect while choring outside the house. You can venture to a laundromat in another neighborhood to wash your blouse <or shirt if you're a guy>. Or maybe you're a guy with a blouse. Clothes are unisex these days and androgyny is all the rave. So grab a blouse, shirt or something else with dirt and wash away. Hang out until it dries and see who you can meet on the fly.

Me personally. I wash clothes every three months, so this P.S. doesn't work for me. It takes too much energy to carry my seven loads down the stairs to my car, so by the time I get to the laundromat I have no energy to connect. So instead I invite friends over on wash days and yes I said *wash days* because it truly is a days-long process. If you recall, I wash clothes every three months and this is not an exaggeration.

I wash clothes when I'm forced to AKA when I run out of undies. A. Because I travel a lot so I'm rarely home and B. Because I hate doing laundry. We all have that one chore that we don't adore and washing clothes is mine. So I make it adorable by turning it into connection time with many friends, many wines and a few whines.

2.17

Improve Your Home

Are you addicted to HGTV like me? If not, try to watch it and you will see why I love this channel so much. Or maybe you won't. It's your prerogative. But I love it and even without a TV, I watch HGTV faithfully. How? It's the number one thing I look forward to when traveling. The number one. Eating new food and seeing new sites are close twos and threes.

So every night while traveling I curl up at the end of the day with the fuzzy robe hanging in the bathroom of my hotel room, fuzzy socks I bring from home and I get my HGTV on. While eating in bed and a bonnet on my head I crash and wake up the next morning with

HGTV still on the TV and the sun peeping through the window to greet me. That's love.

I love HGTV because it feeds my creativity and it inspires me to fix up the home I don't own. That's right, I don't own a TV or a home but in due time. Right now neither are priorities of mine and I can tell you why over a pastry or coffee sometime, but until then let's talk home improvement.

Like HGTV, Home Depot and Lowe's can teach you a thing or two about fixing up the home you have or the home you don't. As you know, I fall in the latter class of non-home ownership but I still love learning how to backsplash. Most, if not all, of these classes are free and you can meet cool and creative peeps.

Let me repeat. These home improvement classes are free and while learning how to fix up your fixer-upper you can meet cool peeps. So try spending a weekend there, or a few weekends there, to learn how to back-splash, drywall and change locks while connecting off the clock.

2.18

Host An Event: At Home

I love to entertain at home. I love to entertain for Movie Mondays, Taco Tuesdays, Wine Down Wednesdays, Think Tank Thursdays, Fondue Fridays, Sangria Saturdays and Soul Food Sundays. I love to entertain at home, I love to eat and I love to meet peeps, and hosting provides great opportunities to do all three.

When I host, I usually tell my friends to invite their friends so we can all be friends. Shout out to Biggie Smalls. Speaking of small, I live in an apartment so my gatherings are quite small. There's nothing biggie about them. I invite two to three peeps at the most and I ask those two to three peeps to bring a peep. As events would have it, if six get invited, only four will show, so I follow the 80/20 rule when being a host

During my busy weeks, I host on Sundays. Sundays are my regular meal-prep days, so I'm cooking anyway. I set a theme and cook a little bit more, so instead of cooking for one I cook for four. But during my not-so-busy weeks I host during the week.

Sometimes I prep the meal ahead of time on Sundays, and other times I cook a quick-and-easy meal the very same day that looks gourmet. A little seasoning here and an herb there can turn a basic meal into 5-star fare. So pick your day, prep your meal, invite some friends and connect and chill.

2.19
Host An Event: Away From Home

I've hosted and co-hosted many events away from home, like luncheons and mixers, fundraisers and happy hours, campaign kickoffs, holiday parties and product samplings with brand ambassadors. Some events paid me and some events just thanked me. Some events sought after me and other events I got randomly.

But regardless of how you score the gig, to host or to co-host an event is a win-win.

Your name gets plastered on everything and I do mean everything: flyers, press releases, emails and magazines. You also get to greet guests on arrival at the door, you get to work the room, schmooze and more. Hosting and co-hosting is perfect for those scared to meet peeps because it forces you out of your comfort zone and draws people to you, making connecting a bit more easy to do.

2.20

Host An Event: Virtually

Virtual happy hours are a new and cool way to meet peeps. You can chill on your couch, eat some treats and meet new peeps virtually. Periscope, Google+ and Zoom make it very easy to host virtual happy hours these days. So pick a date, pick a time, grab some wine and get online. But, and this is a big but, attend one first before you try. Eventbrite and Eventful have them from time to time so search for one and get online.

2.21

Be A Neighbor

"Won't you be my neighbor?" Does this sound familiar? If not, google it. Google it and do it. Mister Rogers encouraged us to do something we should all do—be a neighbor—and the first step to being a neighbor is getting to know the neighbors that we have.

But many of us fail to. Many of us fail to get to know the who or whos living next door. Do you know yours? Do you know who's living next door to you? Do you have the slightest clue? Do you?

Connect and you shall see. It's as easy as 123. Walk, knock and say hello. That's it. It's not like the movies. You don't have to make, bake and take a casserole dish. You can if you wish, but a hello will do. Just say hello and get to know the folks living next door to you.

Speaking of the folks next door, there's an app for this. In fact, there's an app for everything, but the app for this is called Nextdoor. Nextdoor is the ultimate social networking app for neighborhoods. You can connect with the folks next door, the folks next door to them and the folks next door to them. What a gem!

You can even learn about the neighbor that throws the best parties and the neighbor that has nostalgic Halloween candy like Smarties. So download Nextdoor but walk next door too and get to know the folks living next door to you. Toodaloo.

2.22

Walk The Dog

Dogs seek attention. And not a little of it. They seek a lot of it. When they walk, their ears, eyes and tummies say *pat me, rub me, hug me, love me*. And with the wag of a tail, they hypnotize innocent bystanders and cast a "pat me now" spell. Bystanders oblige. They pat, rub, hug and love ears and tummies, especially the ears and tummies of puppies.

I've been under this spell plenty of times and like other innocent bystanders, I oblige. I pat, rub, hug and love the heck out of pets. Maybe because I secretly, but not so secretly, want a pet pup too. Regardless, those puppy dog eyes and wagging tails get me every time. Seriously. Wagging tails will leave you hypnotized and mesmerized and dogs eat up the attention like a prize.

So what is an owner to do while their dog is getting a tummy tickle? Connect. The owner should connect. Tummy tickles are great opportunities to connect, and when you walk your dog you should do just that.

If you don't have a dog, this way can be a bit challenging but not impossible. There are a few solutions that are plausible. You can walk a neighbor's dog or a friend's or you can become a professional dog walker. Professional dog walking can help you make new friends while getting some extra money to spend. Sounds like a win-win friend.

2.23

Exercise

I prefer to get slim without the gym but that's not the healthiest way to be. Plus the gym and other exercise regimen provide ample opportunities to meet peeps. When I do convince myself to exercise, I look for things that don't feel like exercise. I look for things that disguise the cise like cool 5Ks, cycling and hiking mixed with a little bit of yoga, dancing and prancing.

Sometimes I partake alone to see who I can meet and other times I invite folks to come with me. When I invite folks to join, there's a perk—it forces me to go. Otherwise my mind says go to the gym and my heart says get more sleep and eat more ice cream.

My fav is this goat cheese and cherry ice cream from a little shop that just opened a few months ago. Oh how I want to go. I just need a bite, just one bite, a taste if you will. The crave is real and I could eat more ice cream if I exercised more, but I digress for the tenth time today.

Back to getting slim with some type of gym.

Another exercisey way to meet peeps is through an intramural sport of some sort. There's football, kick-ball, volleyball and golf, softball, basketball, tennis and soccer, amongst others. Intramural sports are like sisterhoods and brotherhoods filled with friendly competition that never hurt no body and friendly competition that creates instant camaraderie. So grab your sneaks, compete and go meet some peeps.

P.S. If competition is not your thing and you don't want to be an active member of the team, you can still meet peeps by attending the games or meeting up for drinks. Drinks? Yes drinks. A lot of these teams have social components and they usually meet for drinks after the game to wallow in their sorrow if they lost or rave and praise if they won. It's much fun, so go get you some.

2.24

Get Your Hair Did

There's something special about a barber or beauty shop chair because when you sit in them you spontaneously start telling your business to the person doing your hair. Many personal and professional problems have been discussed and deciphered in the barber and beauty shop: politics, parenting, technology, traveling, religion, relationships and the best chips. If you've never been in one, you're missing a whole lot of, whole lot of, whole lot of fun. But don't fret, the movie *Barber Shop* can give you a sneak-peak into these people-grooming boutiques.

I feel like I'm meeting with a life coach every time I sit in my beautician's chair. She's always asking me what I'm up to and always recommending other clients of hers that I should talk to. Sometimes the other beauticians and clients in the shop chime in too, and I walk out feeling renewed. Hair did. Connecting did. Everything did. You should try it too!

2.25

Be Selfish

Self-care is typically the last thing on our list of things to do, when it should be the first. Oftentimes we feel guilty for indulging in self-care, so it never gets off our to-do list. But right here and right now my friend I am giving you permission to be selfish. To be selfish and indulge in self-care. Not only because it's a MUST but because it's a way to connect while you de-stress.

You can reconnect with old friends and new friends by inviting folks with you. Or. You can connect with the peeps rubbing your feet. Yes I said feet. Which is ironic because I absolutely hate feet. They disgust me, but one of my monthly self-care rituals involves a mani and a pedi. Sometimes I invite folks with me and other times I converse with the pedicurist rubbing my feet.

We swap stories and recipes, remedies and accessories. And just like that we connect. I have connected with many folks in this manner. My eyebrow threader, my makeup artist, my beautician and my masseuse are all friends of mine. All four of them. And now we hang outside of feet rubs and back scrubs, hairdos and eyebrow hues. It's a beautiful thing.

2.26

Attend Church

With the increase of nones—not nuns but nones (people that are nonreligious)—church is becoming less and less frequented. Many are starting to feel less welcomed than welcomed when they step into these four walls and numerous halls. **Side note:** Have you ever gotten lost in a mega-church? OMG. I've been lost to never be found again and to only be found again when the church service ends.

But back to the nones.

People are starting to feel confused and judged by certain teachings and preachings that contradict their own morals, values and beliefs. And this isn't me saying these things…this is research. But I believe—regardless of beliefs or lack thereof—church is still a place to worship, connect and be. So whether you are a nun or a none or something in between, I believe there's a church for everybody and everything.

Now this is my truth and I speak nothing but my truth, so help me God, but I do believe there's a church for everybody and everything. Churches are starting to get innovative and creative to appeal to the needs of the masses. There's warehouse churches, nondenominational churches, churches of Christ, churches of paleontology and churches of Bedside Baptist aka online church. I've attended this church a time or two or three in my life when sick and sleepy. I've also attended when traveling.

I lay in bed with a pillow stuck to my head and stream the service online. It's the best, but my mom still feels *if I can go out on Saturday, then I can get my butt up on Sunday and go to church* <her words not mine>. I've been out of her house for almost 15 years and I can still hear her saying these words loud and clear like she's near and dear. That's the power of fear.

Speaking of power. Superpower—like a shark and bear. Let's not forget about the church of Beyoncé. Seriously. There's a church of Bey created by the almighty beehive. They say slay and I say cray. Now, I'm not judging and I hope you aren't too. We all have our opinions on church like everything else we do. I'm just saying there's a church for everybody and everything. And although I'm not supposed to write about this or politics. I must. This is a book about connecting and church is a place to do just that so hush.

2.27

Be A Member

Joining clubs is easy in grade school, middle school, high school and even college. Well maybe not easy but easier to join than they are in adulthood. From my experience at least. It's easier because the clubs are right there. At school. At campus. At your fingertips.

In adulthood it takes more commitment to join a club. We have to find the time. We have to find the energy. We have to find the monies. And most importantly, we have to find the synergy. We have to find clubs that fit. Fit our interests, fit our lifestyles and fit the question is this worth my while. And I say yes. Clubs are worth your while because clubs help you connect.

The clubs you can join, lead and create in adulthood are endless and I don't know where to begin this list but here goes it:

Affinity Groups	*Chambers/Councils*
Alumni Associations	*Dance Troops*
Boards	*Exercise Groups*
Book Clubs	*Food Clubs*
Church Clubs	*Fraternities & Sororities*
Committees	*Hobby Groups*

Mastermind Groups	Social Groups
Military Groups	Sports Clubs
Political Groups	Travel Groups
Professional Associations & Organizations	Volunteer Groups
	Work Clubs

I'm sure there are many, many, many more you can add too but I hope this list gets things started for you. So join. Join and use the club as an accessible pool of connections. You can connect as a group when the club meets or you can connect one-on-one outside of the club's meetings.

2.28

Run To Reunions

Kinships, fellowships, fraternities and sororities, colleges, universities and high schools all have reunions. Some are monthly, some are yearly and some are every five years. Some bring anxiety, some bring excitement and some bring tears. Some are happy hours, some are retreats, some are trips and some are shop-and-sips. But all of them are opportunities to connect and perfect your who. So go, have fun, grab a bite and reunite.

2.29

Attend A Networking Event

I just gagged when I typed the word networking. I really dislike this word. I won't say hate since my mom is going to read this but just know my dislike is real. Networking is a business card exchange, transactional, take-take-take, quantity not quality, cold and surface. Connecting is story sharing, people caring, relational and reciprocal, give-give-give, quality not quantity, warm and deep.

However, no one says "connecting event," and if I told you to attend a connecting event you wouldn't have a clue as to what to do. So until the world gets my clue (hint hint) I will say networking event.

Now that I have explained myself. Yes. I want you to attend a networking event but I don't want you to network. I want you to connect. I want you to share your who not your do. I want you to connect. I want you to talk about your person not your profession. I want you to connect. I want you to listen to the stories of others and share your own. I want you to connect.

I also want you to go alone. When we don't go alone we tend to stay with the friends we came with and what's the good in that? Go alone or ditch your friends at the door, and when you feel lonely, crash a circle where two to three are gathered.

People don't believe me when I say this, but it's much easier to hold a conversation with a group of people versus one-on-one. So if and when you feel alone or scared to connect—crash a circle. My favorite lines when crashing circles are, *"Hey can I crash your circle?"* Or. *"Can I join your circle?"* And just like that I'm in the circle.

2.30

Put. The. Phone. Down.

Cell phones are barriers, obstacles and walls that prevent connections, so PUT THEM DOWN. I repeat. PUT THEM DOWN and be in the moment. I know it's hard. It's hard for me at times because it's easy to get caught up in email. It's easy to get lost in texts. It's easy to get captivated by likes. Or, the lack there of—especially for pictures and posts you really like that others don't—but I digress. You get the point. Put the phone down and look approachable. Put the phone down and connect.

2.31

Be A Good Samaritan

Be good. Be a Samaritan. And be caring. Because kind acts are not only the right thing to do, kind acts help you connect with people too. Think about it. You can hold a door or carry a bag, point out a clothing snag or tear off a sales tag. You can help someone up a hill, buy someone a meal, pick up and hand someone their dropped bank bill, return a license or hand someone a tissue while they cry in silence. Helping thy neighbor is a love of labor that can yield much-needed mends and new friends.

Volunteer Or Be Voluntold

There's no shortage of volunteer activities, as you may very well know. Daily I'm asked to volunteer and daily I'm being voluntold. Can you relate? With full plates it's easy to say no to these requests these days, but I encourage you to say yes. I encourage you to say yes and connect.

Volunteering looks way different than it used to be. Organizations like United Way and Ronald McDonald House are creating programs for working professionals that make volunteering easy-peasy. There's no application and there's no orientation. All you have to do is sign up and show up. It's a breeze!

You can commit one hour one day a month or one day a year, and after volunteering the volunteers usually meet up for connecting and beer like Cheers. There are many volunteer programs like this around, so find the one that fits your needs in your own town. If you have more capacity to give your time, talents and treasures— woohoo. There are many associations, organizations and boards that could use this too.

P.S. In addition to volunteering for nonprofits, you can also volunteer at conferences and at work too. You can volunteer to take the lead on something or volunteer to do the thing no one else wants to do. This will give you quick exposure too and another opportunity to meet folks that are new.

Donate Dollars

If you absolutely cannot volunteer your time and talents, volunteer your treasures. In addition to being a good way to help your community, donating dollars is a good way to meet peeps. Wondering how, since you're donating your treasures not your time? Well, most charities and nonprofits have thank-you events for their donors and they are fun. Fun in the sun fun. I've been to wine and cheese soirées, ballgames, jazz concerts and house parties around the holidays. Best of all, they are Free99, they are for a great cause, they tend to have great people and they usually have great wines. Exactly what I call a great time!

2.34

Gala Hop

I don't know about you, but I love to play dress-up. I love to dress up, I love to clean up and I clean up very well if I do say so myself. I'm sure the same is true for you. You may not like dressing up like I do, but I'm sure you clean up well too, and galas are picture-perfect opportunities to dress up, clean up and meet up.

The meeting and greeting you can do at galas is two thumbs up because gala committees do all they can do to get the who of whos in one room. All you have to do is show up, be you and schmooze. That's it. So dust off your cocktail attire and your after-five flair, practice your story and galatize your hair. I love galas, so I may see you there. But beware. Galas can get expensive, especially the upper-echelon charity and celebrity galas.

Tickets can range from $50 to $25,000 and sometimes even more. Yes I said more. The more expensive the ticket, the more exclusive the people, the place, the food and the décor. If you want exclusivity, be prepared to pay more or know someone at the door. You can also volunteer or find someone with an extra ticket to give. I believe in you friend and I believe you can get in, so good luck on your quest. I wish you the best.

2.35
Take A Stand

Social issues and political races create spaces to make the world a better place while connecting with new faces. You can help run a campaign, advocate or demonstrate. You can organize, synthesize or strategize. You can facilitate, motivate or activate. You can speak, donate or document. You get the hint. You can plug in—in many ways on any given day. So take a stand and lend a hand while making new friends.

Part Three: Work

In the words of Rihanna, work, work, work, work, work is something that most of us know all too well. Far too well. And regrettably, work can get in the way of connecting. At least we like to think so, but it doesn't always have to. So use the ways below and get to know the folks working directly or indirectly with you.

Commute

If you can commute—commute. It reduces the carbon footprint and makes for a perfect connection blueprint. From carpools and planes to Ubers and trains, I've made many a friends while commuting. Reason friends, season friends and lifetime friends. Prima donna-ist friends, honest friends and adventure friends. Nice friends, wise friends and nothing but business friends. Different friends, mentor friends and friends to the end. I've made many a friends.

I've made many a friends and I've made many a commutes. I've made so many commutes in my non-suits and boots that I am now an Uber VIP. A proud member of the Uber VIP elite. But I have no clue what any of that even means other than the fact that I've given Uber too much green. But money aside, I've made many a friends during my Uber rides. So download the app, the first ride is free, hop on in and see who you can meet. P.S. You can also use Lyft if you choose.

Be Communal

Many coffee shops have communal tables, making it easy to drink and meet, eat and meet or in my case eat and drink and meet. I go to coffee shops a lot to get coffee and set up shop. Coffee shops are my workspace, my third place and my home base. Coffee shops are my one-stop shop to get caffeine, peep the scene and meet new peeps.

You must admit. The people-watching at coffee shops is the best. The best! But I highly advise you to give people-watching a rest for just a sec. Speak to the people you meet. Don't just peep. Say hello too and get to know the folks sitting or standing next to you.

In other words, I want you to channel your inner communal coffee connecting. What the what? Communal coffee connecting: the art of meeting new peeps while drinking caffeine. Try saying that three times fast. Communal coffee connecting. Communal coffee connecting. Communal coffee connecting.

I just tried and it was bad. Real bad. Hard to say but easy to do. I promise you. First you must order coffee. Second you must sit. Third you must talk and that's it. That is it. Order coffee, sit at a communal table and exchange dialogue with the people next to you. That's communal coffee connecting.

I know. I know. Communal tables can make us feel weird and out of place since many of us like our own personal space. But communal tables are the best way to chat, chit and shoot the _____ < *insert rhyming word here* >.

1. *Politics*

2. *S****

3. *Bricks*

4. *Cake Mix*

Speaking of cake mix—here's the icing on the cake. Coffee shops that have communal tables typically have good vibes only. Now, I doubt there's a scientific study to prove the correlation between communal tables and good vibes, but it sounds like a good correlation to me.

To further my belief, I believe good-vibe-only places and spaces attract a customer base of good-vibe-only peeps that are willing and ready to mix and meet. So move your feet and find your seat at a communal coffee table in a city near you. Or. A restaurant near you, since restaurants are starting to subscribe to the communal dining concept too.

3.38
Mentor And Be Mentored

When people hear the word mentor, they get scared. Not because they don't care but because of the time they have to spare. Mentor has become synonymous with time commitment and for this reason many people are starting to resent it. But mentorship can be whatever two peeps decide it should be. It can be a check-in here or a cup of coffee there. It can be a weekly, monthly or even quarterly frequency. Again, it can be anything two peeps decide it should be.

So call it something else if you want, pick your frequency and get to mentoring. You can mentor someone you know or someone new, and while mentoring, you should be mentored too. Just do it. No more excuses and no more shooting mentorship the deuces.
Just do it.

Many employers, organizations and associations have mentor programs to make mentorship that much easier for you. I've been in a few of these as a mentor and as a mentee. Two with work, one with a women's professional organization and another with a young professional's association. Each process was easy-peasy and each process was stress-free.

I filled out a quick one-pager outlining my goals and future roles of interest. Then I was matched to a mentor or mentee that fit my wish list. From there we determined our level of commitment, and the experiences were splendid! Each time I met someone new and each time I learned something new. So again call it what you want to, but you should do it too.

3.39
Be A Buddy

Growing up, my brother had a My Buddy and I had a Kid Sister. We loved those freakin' dolls. I can even hear the tune of the commercial playing in my head as we speak. But recently I googled My Buddy and the pictures of that doll scared the heck out of me! They were scary. Really scary. Not sure why I wasn't scared at 3. Maybe I'm scared now because of Chucky. IDK but I do know that being the non-doll version of a buddy can be a great way to meet some peeps.

So what is a non-doll version of a buddy? Well. It's a work companion. A work companion that supports onboardings by welcoming new employees. Some companies leave this to human resources, some operations and some administrative assistants. Others leave this to employees that volunteer to assist.

I've been a buddy voluntarily and involuntarily, formally and informally, when I was officially called a buddy and when I was called nothing. I've been a My Buddy and a Kid Sister to plenty and by being one I've met plenty of peeps.

I met some by simply welcoming them on their first day and walking them to their seats. I met some by being a resource they could call upon their first week. And I met some by buying them their first lunch—on the company of course.

As you can see, being a buddy has its perks, privileges and benefits, so be a buddy to a new employee, and if your company doesn't have a buddy program— start one.

3.40
Take Breaks

I travel a ton these days, but when I work in the office, I take breaks. A lot of breaks. At least three to five a day. And when I take breaks, I take the long way. I take the long way and I alternate. I walk one way to the kitchen and another way back. I walk one way to the bathroom and another way back. I walk, talk, chat and connect.

On my way to and from, I say hello to everyone I pass. This allows me to catch up with folks, say a few jokes and get to know the ghosts of my colleagues' past.

Seriously. These breaks are like dates. They are mini speed-dates that give me the opportunity to get to know the people working next to me. An opportunity to get to know the person behind the profession.

A side we rarely show those we spend so much of our time and lives with because many believe befriending colleagues is a cardinal sin. A deadly sin that should be forbidden. And I should know because I used to be one of these peeps. One of these peeps used to be me. But now I believe the opposite to be true. I believe your colleagues can be close friends too, so take breaks, walk the room and get to know the people working next to you.

Note: Some companies don't do breaks. Not as many as I take anyway. Some will even discipline those that leave their seats "too much." So be aware. Be very aware of the spoken and unspoken work rules you may have to adhere to and inform your boss if you feel the need to. She/he can approve and recommend more peeps for you to schmooze.

3.41
Arrive Early

Meetings create countless chances to…well…meet, so arrive early. When you arrive early, you can converse and connect with other early birds too. I've made some of my best connections with colleagues at meetings. I also stay a few minutes after the meeting is over to chat more instead of beelining to the door. In addition to meetings, arrive early to workshops, to conferences, and to speaker series too. The early bird gets the worm, the good snacks, the good seat and time to mix and meet.

3.42

Brown Bag It

As I mentioned earlier—I travel a ton. At least once every two weeks. But my travel comes and goes in peaks. When I'm in the office, I make it a point to schedule quarterly lunches with me. That's right. I schedule lunches with Keish. And that's what I call them.

I send an email invite to my entire office and I ask all of my colleagues to eat with me. I reserve a conference room and then instruct everyone to brown bag it. The lunches last an hour and they are the absolute best. We talk, we laugh, we eat and de-stress.

Note: This way tends to work best in small office settings, but it can work in large settings too. Just invite your department to eat with you.

3.43

Attend A Work Event

Many despise work events. Not because they despise their co-workers. But because they despise everything work events represent. Less time with family and more time with colleagues, less time talking big and more time talking small, less time at home and more time talking about work away from work. And lastly, less time relaxing and more time uptighting. But work events don't have to be like this!

I hijack my work events all the time. All of the time. I get people talking about their stories instead of the weather and climbing the corporate ladder. I also invite friends with me, which helps break the ice and adds a little spice. So change your tude toward work events, talk about your who not your do and connect like this book teaches you how to.

P.S. You should also attend the work events of friends—especially friends that work in different industries than you do. You can learn something new and meet new people too.

3.44
Learn A Language

Nelson Mandela said it best: "Without language, one cannot talk to people and understand them; one cannot share their hopes and aspirations, grasp their history, appreciate their poetry, or savor their songs."

In other words, language is essential to connecting, and knowing more than one is not only an asset, it's a magnet. If you haven't tried to learn a new language— try it. Whether you use textbooks or audio books, online classes or language exchanges, language lessons can and will increase your perceptions and your connections.

3.45
Get PD

PD, better known as professional development, is an awesome way to meet people while bettering yourself at the same time. Me personally. I participate in at least one professional development program outside of work each year. This ranges from workshops to speaker series, shadowing and everything in between. Each program provides new comprehensions and new connections…but these PDS can get expensive.

The going rate, these days, seems to be $5,000 and up for a yearlong PD. But I always check for scholarships before I pay. If I can't get a scholarship, I ask to shadow a few sessions for free. If that doesn't work, I ask for work-study and I usually get one of the three. So use PD to meet some peeps but check to see if you can get it for free.

3.46
Be A Fellow

Fellowships are the bees-knees. You get PD and you get to meet peeps. And not just peeps that live in your neck of the woods but peeps that live in the necks of other woods too. It's the truth! I absolutely love fellowships, and there are two that I would really like to do: Aspen and Eisenhower. So if you know the people in power, holler at your girl.

These two fellowships can change my world and yours too if you haven't already been through. Any who. Back to you. Oh wait. New Profit is on my list too. Ok. Ok. Now really back to you.

Join a fellowship in a town near you to learn as much as you can learn and meet as much as you can meet. I've done three and have met some pretty amazing peeps. The fellowships even have GroupMe's to stay in touch and quarterly happy hours to catch up.

3.47
Take A Class

Some days I just want to relive my college days. I ate better, I worked out more and class was a few feet away from my dorm room door. College was the life. And it still can be your life if you want it to be. Well some of it. Many colleges and universities are now offering continuing education classes like speaker and lecture series. They can be free or for a nominal fee. Either way it's a good way to meet peeps.

Some companies will even pay for continuing education and advanced degrees. It's usually a part of your benefits package, so look and see. If you can get free education, why not take advantage? It's a win-win. You can learn new knowledge and meet new friends.

3.48
Be Entrepreneurial

Clarification. You do not have to be an entrepreneur to be entrepreneurial. There is such a thing as intrapreneurship. Whether you own your own business or work for someone else, the ability to solve problems and be innovative are good skills to have. Curiosity may kill the cat but innovation can bring it back.

Innovation can also be a really cool way to meet some really cool peeps doing really cool thangs, and gangs of innovation communities are popping up everywhere. And when I say everywhere, I do mean everywhere. There are innovation trips and fellowships, meetups and collaborative workspaces, accelerators and incubators—you name it, innovation has it.

I'm in an innovation space weekly, from Venture Café to House of Genius to 1 Million Cups, and all are great places to be, think and meet peeps:

- *Venture Café is a weekly innovation meetup that brings together more than 500 peeps a week. And it's free! I repeat. It's free. Currently it's only in five cities, but its presence is growing.*

- *House of Genius is in more than 30 cities and brings a dozen entrepreneurs and innovators together to mix and meet.*

- *1 Million Cups is in more than 100 cities and brings together three to five entrepreneurs weekly to pitch their ideas and get feedback from their community.*

All three places are safe and inclusive spaces to meet new faces. All three places are creative and collaborative spaces to connect with new faces. All three spaces, and many others like them, are waiting for you to share your who not your do. So go bond. And in the words of

Buzz Lightyear's brother, "To entrepreneurship and beyond."

3.49

Work. Work. Work. Work. Work.

The sharing economy has made having a second job quite attractive. There's Airbnb, Uber, Lyft, DogVacay, TaskRabbit and many more like it. The sharing economy allows you to rent out things you already own, from brownstones to drones. And over the past few years this type of economy has grown and grown and grown. More people renting means more people mingling. Or at least it should. So rent your extra room or drive for Uber—at least one day a week—and see how many people you can meet.

Part Four: Play

Wanna play? Of course you do. Adults should play too because playing increases creativity and connectivity. So the lesson of today—work smarter and play harder. Okay. Kay. Kay. Shout-out to Lil Scrappy.

4.50

Be A Fan

Are you an enthusiast, devotee, admirer, lover or supporter of any person, place or thing? In other words, are you a fan? From sports teams to concerts, Ted Talks to Kickstarts, parties and everything in between, there's usually a fan corps or a street team. Fan corps and street teams are like work-study. The fan pubs the event via gorilla marketing and social media tactics and in return she/he gets free tickets to the event.

Just know there's levels to this. The fan has to sell X amount of tickets, post X number of tweets or distribute X fliers but you get the gist. I say all of this to say— the fan corps and street team can fund your fun and be a fun way to meet peeps. So the next time you get ready to RSVP, check to see if your person, place or thing has a street team.

4.51

Fulfill Your Fantasy

Fantasy leagues are imaginary sports teams that fans can own, manage and coach to compete against other fans. It also doubles as a way to meet new friends. And like fantasy leagues, fantasy video games double as the same.

Some leagues and games will even have meetups to kick off the season, so go play games to your heart's desire. You now have a reason. Joking. Please don't play fantasy leagues and games all day. Please. I don't want you to get in trouble with your boo. Just play for an hour or two and get to know the folks playing along with you.

4.52
Watch TV

TV shows aren't TV shows anymore. TV shows are drama series equipped with clothing lines, soundtracks and backpacks that make crowds go wild. A true life-style. People wait impatiently for premieres and set reminders on their phones. They even head to happy hours and house parties on premiere nights so they don't have to watch alone. They tweet about their favorite scenes and characters too—creating multiple opportunities to connect with fellow watchers old and new.

You too can join the TV show thrill by hosting your own Netflix and Chill. But if the thought of hosting a watch night makes you want to shrill, there's a neigh-borhood bar that will. So make your way there and connect with your TV show family over food, drinks and "what do you thinks." But beware. Some bars have no-talking rules. Not all of the time. Just during the show. So you may have to show up early to connect if you decide to go. Just thought you should know.

4.53

Be Social

Friend. It's time to have a heart-to-heart. A serious heart-to-heart. And I want you to be honest. Honest with yourself and honest with me. Really honest. I want transparent honesty. Ready?

Are you the friend that always stands people up? Like always. Like all of the time always. Are you that person?

Are you the person that makes plans to hang with friends and then on the day in question you don't show up because you're asleep or on Netflix and chilling? If so, stop. Stop it friend. Stop being the friend that stands people up. <Insert clapping noise here to emphasis this sentence>. And if you have no clue what the heck clapping has to do with anything, reread the sentence and clap when you say every syllable. Let's try.

Stop. Being. The. Friend. That. Stands. People. Up.

See the difference? See the emphasis? Stop being this friend. Stop being the friend that never goes out and about. If you don't change your ways, you will soon be the friend that stops getting invited out.

I'm the friend that's the complete opposite. I say yes to everything. Every single thing. Every single social thing to a fault. I spend many nights trying to figure out how to manage my double and triple bookings. Some nights I manage them well and some nights I manage them not so well but every night I say yes, I connect. I connect with old friends, new friends, borrowed and blue friends, and you should too friend. So be social and stop being solo dolo.

4.54
Take A Shot

T-Pain likes the bartender and so should you. And while liking the bartender, like the DJ too. Bartenders and DJs know people. A lot of people. And they can introduce you to people. A lot of people. So how do you befriend these two?

You can chat with the bartender while she/he is mixing your drink—or drinks, no judgment—and with the DJ while she/he is spinning your tunes. But beware. Bartenders and DJs are busy folks, so be strategic when you approach. If you try to talk at the wrong time, you can quickly move from being a friend to being a frenemy.

You can also meet these peeps by attending their events. Some bartenders teach mixology classes while others host cocktail bashes for the masses. Me personally, I prefer the classes. You can hone your mixing skills, learn a side hustle to pay the bills and mix and mingle in a more intimate setting.

And like bartenders, DJs host events and teach classes too. To find out if a DJ teaches class, just attend one of their events, request a song and ask. I've taken multiple classes from multiple DJs and now I have a DJ name. That's right. An official fo shizzle DJ name.

Are ya'll ready for this???

K Slay. And for the record, I had this name before Bey's Lemonade. All love no shade. I love Bey all day every day and one day K Slay on the 1s and 2s will be coming soon to a city near you.

4.55
Be A Regular

Have you ever been somewhere where everybody knows your name? If not you're missing out and you should get a piece of this clout. Frequenting a local spot will get you on the VIP list, so become a regular and enjoy this bliss.

You can be a regular anywhere and everywhere. At bars, lounges, restaurants and the like. But my favorite place to be a regular is at trivia night.

I will be the first to say I am terrible at this. I am never smarter than a 5th grader and I am not exaggerating. I am oh so serious. No ifs, ands or buts about it. Trivia night is not my friend and my team never wins. But the beer, mulligans and crazy crowds make connecting with folks so much fun, so drive on over and get you some.

4.56
Be The Third Wheel

Being the third wheel has such a negative connotation, but I'm the third wheel all the time. All of the time. But before you give me a side-eye...let...me...explain. I

don't crash dates. Well some, but not romantic relationship dates. I crash friend dates and I also eat off
people's plates but that's a topic for another conversation. Back to the crashing and dinner dashing.

It usually looks something like this. It's Friday and I'm
chatting with a friend or colleague about their weekend
plans. You know the convo…

FRIEND: Hey. How are you? How was your week?

ME: It was good. Crazy busy. So glad it's Friday!

FRIEND: Me too. What are you doing this weekend?

ME: I need to adult—clean, wash clothes, run errands
and cook. What about you?

FRIEND: I have some friends coming in town today. We
are going to a wine and cheese tasting tonight and a
brunch tomorrow.

MY THOUGHTS: Wine, cheese and brunch sounds way
better than adulting. A heck of a lot better.

ME: Oh cool…I wanna go.

And just like that I've invited myself to someone else's
friend date. However, this way doesn't always work.
Sometimes tickets have already been purchased for
activities, so it's not so easy to add a third wheel. But
most of the time it works, and adding a third wheel can
even lower the bill. A pizza split between three, for
example—I love pizza—is cheaper than a pizza split
between two, so being the third wheel makes economic
sense too.

4.57

Date Yourself

I date myself monthly. Not because I'm single and trying to mingle but because I adore the art of explore. So like Dora, minus the backpack and Boots, I explore. Every month I try one new adventure alone to prove to myself that I'm bad to the bone. I've done a DJ lesson, an improv session, skydiving, flying, zip-lining, computer coding, poetry, karaoke, photography and graffiti. I've done painting and pottery, arts and crafts, jewelry making and dessert baking. I've even done a sewing class that I didn't pass.

But pass or fail, each adventure has stretched me like a Capstone. Pass or fail, each adventure has pushed me out of my comfort zone. Pass or fail, each adventure has connected me with weird peeps, and I love weird peeps. I love weird peeps and I love geeks. I'm a weird peep and a chic geek so I love to meet other weird peeps and geeks—plus or minus the chic.

Weird peeps and geeks are distinct and diverse, innovative and creative. In short, weird peeps and geeks are dope. Yes. I still say dope—it's the 80's in me. And in true 80's form of play—I dare you to date yourself, and if dares don't work for you—Simon says, *"Life should be full of play and fun, so go play, have fun and meet someone."*

4.58
Dabble In This And That PLAY

Dabble.com is a dabbleicious (made-up word) way to experience a city and meet new peeps. You can attend classes taught by local residents from soap making to break dancing. Or. You can share your passion with others by teaching your own class. It's a win-win full of zen-zen and friendly friends. But Dabble.com isn't the only way to experience or experiment in a city. You can try your hand at some of the apps below to meet new peeps while on the go.

When I first moved to St, Louis, I became a Groupon groupie. Like seriously friend. A groupie, an addict, a Groupon fanatic. I had to call myself on a Friday afternoon, invite myself over in a weird creepy voice, sit myself down and have a true intervention with me, myself and I.

My Groupon addiction was worse than some folks' QVC addictions. I was ordering things I had no use for. It went from me ordering classes to connect to me ordering sheep fur pillows for my neck. I was a true wreck and I have the receipts to prove it.

On the flip side, I met so many cool peeps going to Groupon classes and Meetup meets and many of these peeps are still friends with me. That's right. They've been putting up with my silliness for six years. The thought of it kind of makes me want to shed a tear. A real tear. A real single tear like BuzzFeed's 11 Most

Powerful Single Tears Ever Shed article. It's an oldie but goodie and a true must-read.

But back to dabbling, grouponing and meeting up. Get out of the house, spend a few bucks and see who you can meet. BUT don't become a groupie. I repeat. Meet but don't become a Groupon groupie that needs interventions and recovery. Just buy classes to connect and stay away from the sheep fur pillows for your neck.

Apps from left to right/top to bottom—Groupon, Living Social, Yelp, Meetup, Eventful and Eventbrite.

4.59

Parking Lot Pimp

When I was too young to do anything but school and too broke to do anything that was cool—my friends and

I would parking lot pimp. We would get dropped off or crowd in the only friend's car that drove and post up at cool places and cool spaces. We would do this religiously. Almost every weekend. Literally.

Sometimes we would parking lot pimp at the mall or the park. Other times we would parking lot pimp at the skating rink. Then there were times when we would parking lot pimp at restaurants after grabbing a bite to eat. But our favorite spaces and places to parking lot pimp were at events and dances we were too young or too broke to attend. We would post up in the car or outside of the car—in the parking lot—until the event or dance let out just to see how many new or old friends we could scout.

Now that I'm older my parking lot pimping days are over. Well kinda. They are over in that sense anyway. Now I'm old enough and financially stable enough to go to the wheres I want to go, do the whats I want to do, see the things I want to see and be at the places I want to be. And. I'm no longer limited by transportation to and from cool places and cool spaces.

The goal is still the same though. Go out and see how many new or old friends I can scout. But instead of posting up in the parking lot I tend to post up at hot spots. In the Lou there's this neat innovation community called the Cortex. One day I posted up there for an hour and met more than 15 peeps while reading. 15 peeps.

Other days, when I'm not sleepy, I will post up after events. I will mix and mingle at the bar, I will mix and mingle while waiting on my valeted car or I will mix and mingle while grabbing a late-night bite to eat. Occasionally, I will do all three if I ate my Wheaties and have the energy. So eat your Wheaties and find some places and spaces to post up and meet some new faces.

4.60

Take A Trip

Travel is a great way to expand your horizons, try bold foods like bison, develop shared understandings and see scenery that's simply outstanding. Travel is also a marvelous way to make friends. You can make friends on the plane, on the train, in the custom line and while you wine and dine.

My job takes me on the road and in the air almost weekly so this way comes easy to me. But for peeps that don't travel for work like I do, don't worry be happy because I have some travel tips, tricks and tidbits to help you:

1. *Travel during slow seasons and low seasons like fall and winter.*

2. *Use travel apps and websites to catch flight deals, steals and thrills like Google Flights, The Flight Deal, Hopper, Airfordable, Skiplagged, Secret Flying and Skyscanner.*

3. *Follow travel groups on social media to take advantage of group travel specials.*

4. *Stay at Airbnbs or with friends.*

5. *Volunteer and travel for free with programs like WWOOF.*

6. *Teach English overseas.*

7. *Do a culture exchange like Fulbright or the like.*

8. *Save and go. Just simply get up and go.*

I have met some of my best friends on the road and in the air. I met one of my good friends in Puerto Rico a few years ago when my mom and I were traveling for our annual mother-daughter trip. I met another good friend on a cruise ship and another good friend on a bench at South by Southwest® while deciding what to eat.

Funny thing. I met all three friends while hangry. Hangry is three levels above hunger. It's the moment when hunger turns into anger. If you haven't been there—good for you. I meet my hangry hulk almost daily and it causes me to act extremely shady until food gets in my belly. But on these three days my hangry hulk was a bit less shady and more of a lady. On these three days my hangry hulk kept calm, making it easy to meet peeps while looking for street eats.

4.61

Staycate

I just told you to vacate, but when you can't vacate—staycate. Get a map from the welcome center and act like a tourist in your own city. Take alternative routes, try new restaurants, gas up at new stations and head to new locations. Hang out in Greek Town, Chinatown, Little Africa and Little Italy. Hang with yuppies, hang with hippies and hang with historians to learn your city's history. Check out the local museums and catch a band at the local coliseum. Tour new streets, try new treats, savor new sweets and seek new peeps to meet.

4.62
Play And Date

I don't have kids but I have friends that do and play dates make for great ways to meet folks too. Play dates can be birthday parties. They can be walks in the park. They can be sleepovers and movie matinees, ice cream socials and game days. Play dates are for kids in theory, but the parents always have more fun. Especially the ones I've been to when the kids have their juice and the parents have theirs too!

Part Five: Connect

Now that you've lived, worked and played, here's a few more connection ways to try during your 100 days. But these ways are going to require a little more time, patience and perseverance. And some may even require a clearance, an appearance and a dash of coherence. Nonetheless you got this, so get ready, get set and connect.

5.63

Get Awarded

Get awarded but don't wait for others to nominate you. You nominate you and ask others to nominate you too. But make it a cool, calm and collected process for your nominators. To do so—keep a brag sheet. A one-pager with noteworthy things you've done for your company, your industry and your community. Use this brag sheet as a starting point for self-nominations and send it to your peers for peer-nominations.

Once the awards start rolling around, you'll be the talk of the town. Awards are like PR agents, because they get people to notice you. The more awards you get, the more exposure you get. The more exposure you get, the more chances to connect you get. Catch my drift? Awards open doors and awards make people interested in who you are. People will start to seek you out and people will even start to notice you when you're out and about.

But some word of advice. Please make sure you have an updated headshot before you start nominating yourself for awards and getting others to nominate you too. A picture is worth a thousand words and some pictures don't shed the best light on you. Seriously. I've seen so many bad award pictures and I do mean bad. Heck. I even have a few of my own and they never go away.

Those bad pictures haunt me like Groundhog Day. The movie not the holiday. They show up in Google Images and press releases. Friends text them to me with bad-picture teases. They are truly the worst but can be avoided. Just hire a photographer before your bad pictures get exploited.

5.64

Get Featured

Features are freakin' incredible. Recently I got featured on a lifestyle blog that had more than 50 thousand followers! Fifty thousand. 5. 0. Whoa. So how do features work? Well. Content creators and curators, like bloggers and editors, are constantly seeking ways to create and curate content. Content inspiration and motivation is something they seek daily. And I do mean daily.

They seek inspiration and motivation from the daily news, headlines, hot topics, pop culture, politics, entertainment, travel and style. They even seek op-ed and guest features every once in awhile. To submit content, you simply fill out a form on their website or email them your pitch. They will respond if they like what they see and they won't if they don't. If they do, they will send more instructions to you like deadlines and guidelines to get the most readers for your feature.

Then you wait. You submit your article or post and wait. You wait for the release. Then you thank. You thank the powers that be. Then you share. You share it on your feeds. Then you connect. You connect with the people that read.

5.65
Seek Spotlight

CONNECT

Associations, organizations, networks and colleges love opportunities to spotlight their members, employees and alumni. Not to make you look good. More so to make them look good. So make them look good. Send the webmaster, the newsletter editor and the alumni affairs director your good news! New promotion, new award, new degree, new board—all of the new news pertaining to you. They will typically ask you for a headshot, so go ahead and send that too.

I've been spotlighted in everything: department newsletters, company commercials, board bulletins, university quarterlies, professional publications, pamphlets, websites, business journals and more. As you can probably see, there are limitless ways to be spotlighted, so go get your spot and wait for the connections to flock.

5.66
Ask Questions

I always ask questions. Always. At workshops. At conferences. At speaker series and development sessions. At every event, meeting and lesson. If there's a Q&A—I have a question.

If I know the topic of the event and the speaker speaking, I usually come prepared with two to three questions. If I don't know the topic of the event or the speaker speaking, I formulate two to three questions during the event by observing the speaker to see what makes her/him tick. What makes their face smirk and what makes their ears perk. These are the things I look for when formulating my questions and these are the things that make an impression.

Once formulated, my goal is to be the first person to ask the first question. I do this to make myself even more memorable and to guarantee my question hasn't already been asked. One time I got $100 for asking the first question. One hundred whole dollars from a speaker that was the vice president of human resources for a fortune 500 company.

He finished his spiel, opened the floor and asked for questions. To my surprise, it was silent. Like crickets silent. Like crickets crickets silent. Not sure why we say things twice to emphasize it, but it works. It was crickets crickets silent and I was happy. Happy that I didn't have to compete with someone else to be first. So when the floor opened for questions, I stood up with my Wonder Woman confidence and asked my half-formulated question.

Yes. I said half-formulated. I was late to the workshop that day for some reason I can't remember, so I missed my opportunity to observe the vp's ticks, smirks and perks. But I'm a risk-taker, so I took a risk. Heck. A half of a question is better than no question at all.

And to my surprise, he liked my question. I know this because he said, *"Good question."* Then. To my surprise again, he answered my question, walked toward me, reached in his pocket, pulled out a $100 dollar bill and handed it to me. Just like that. It was a true Rick James moment or maybe it was a Dave Chappelle spoof of a

Rick James moment. Either way, I felt rich.

After the workshop I approached the VP to say thank you, as I do with every speaker I hear speak, but this approach wasn't just a thank you for speaking. It was also a thank you for the green. For the one hundred new dollars tugging at my purse strings.

The VP thanked me in return for being brave, handed me his business card and told me to circle back in three weeks to meet. Three weeks came and went twice before we met but when we finally met, it was time well spent. We talked about our stories, our glory, our goals and our roles. And now we meet quarterly, so the moral of this story—it pays to be first.

The second moral of this story—always aim for first, but if first is taken—aim for second, and if second is taken—aim for third. The point. Get in a word. Your word. Preferably during Q&A, but sometimes you have to catch the speaker after the workshop, session or lesson. If and when this is the case, you want to strive to be the first person in the speaker line because these lines can get long. Long long. Longer than Black Friday and longer than free giveaways.

In the event the line is too long, you can also try your hand at emailing the speaker. It's a long shot but still worth a shot. Just email them with the subject line—greetings from xyz event—and in the body of the email, ask your question. Be sure to thank them for their session too. Then follow them on social media, @them and ask your question again. Repetition usually wins because it's a numbers game. The more times a speaker sees your name, the more likely they are to engage. And when they engage, try to find a way to meet face-to-face, especially if you live in the same place.

Another way to catch a speaker is after her/his session, like in the hallway, at a meal or before her/his next session if she/he has a next session. I've even caught up with a few speakers at the bar, others at the workshop after-party and some at the after-after-party. Yes…they party! Don't forget they are humans too. They just tend to know more people than we do.

In addition to the speaker, connecting with the other folks in the room is important too. There are two ways in which one can do this. Well maybe more than two, but I have two favs:

FAV WAY NUMBER ONE:
Volunteer to be the group scribe if small-group work is involved. Many strive to be the group leader, but the leader isn't always the reader. Meaning the group leader isn't always the one reporting out to the bigger group. This job is usually given to the scribe because the scribe is the holder of the information.

Remember, connecting is twofold. Connecting is having the courage to approach peeps AND connecting is creating opportunities for peeps to approach thee. So scribe and share to get your name and face out there.

FAV WAY NUMBER TWO:
Introduce yourself every time you speak, every time you ask a question, every time you scribe and share, every time you say anything. So what does any of this even mean? Well, before

saying anything, I always do three things. I state my name, I say hello and I state a goal.

For example, I say, "Hello everyone, my name is Keisha Mabry and I'm really excited to learn more about the social marketing strategies of others in the room. My question. What percentage of your total budget should your social marketing budget be and how do you spend these funds effectively?"

This opens up my question to not only be answered by the speaker but to also be answered by other leaders in the room. Some folks shoot me a side-eye for being an over-achiever. But many approach me after the workshop, session or lesson with tips, tricks and tidbits in response to my question—and I always love their suggestions. So the moral of this confession—ask and you shall receive connections.

5.67

Ask For Connections

I meet a lot of peeps through peeps. Friends of friends, co-workers of co-workers, classmates of classmates and teammates of teammates. Most of the time peeps just introduce me to peeps or they just recommend peeps for me to meet. But when they don't. I. Just. Ask.

I ask at the end of meetings. I ask peeps on LinkedIn to link me. I ask in Facebook and Twitter posts and I even ask event hosts. I. Just. Ask. I ask and I receive. Don't believe me? Try and see. But before you do, be sure to be specific about the connections you want others to introduce you to.

Here's my method to crowdsourcing my connections:

- *At the end of in-person meetings, my ask typically sounds something like this: "Thank you so much for meeting with me today. I really enjoyed our conversation on social marketing. Hey, do you know any other folks I can chat with to learn about other social marketing strategies?" If the person says yes, I will ask her/him to make the introduction for me and will even offer to write a ghost email for them. The key is to make the job of your connectors as stress-free as possible.*

- *The same holds true for social media asks, and my social media asks usually sound something like: "Hey Facebook and Twitter Friends. I'm shopping around for SEO companies. Do any of you awesome folks have expertise in SEO or know peeps that do? If so, please post a comment on my wall or DM me. Thanks Friends." Then I wait. Some friends will just comment on my wall and others will DM me the peeps I should meet. But recently, Facebook added a recommendation feature, making crowdsourcing that much easier.*

- *At events, I ask the hostess with the mostest to connect me. The hostess invited everyone to the event, so she/he knows the peeps to meet. At events, my ask generally sounds something like this: "Hey friend. Thanks so much for inviting me." Then there's a hug and a handoff of the hostess gift, if I remembered to grab one! If I didn't remember to grab a hostess gift or if I didn't have time to grab a hostess gift, there's usually an apology for my bad friendshipness. And then there's a hug.*

After the hug, I thank the hostess again for the invite and then I respectfully excuse myself to mix and meet with other peeps. But before leaving, I always ask the hostess if there are any peeps they think I should meet. Like this: "Hey friend. Thanks again for the invite. I'm going to grab a drink and mix and meet. Anybody in social marketing you think I should speak with?" If there are peeps I should meet, the hostess will usually walk with me and introduce me. And just like that, a question has led to a connection.

5.68
Seize The Connection

Sometimes you gotta seize the connection. Carpe the connection. Seizing the connection means taking advantage of odd opportunities to connect. It means always being prepared to connect and always being ready to connect. I'll give you an example.

Last year I completed a business fellowship with a cohort of 60 astonishing peeps, and to celebrate this accomplishment, the organization held a graduation ceremony for us. The ceremony was well attended by local leaders, over-achievers, CEOS and the like.

While waiting in line to get my certificate of completion, I noticed a familiar face in my peripheral. My peripheral friend. And the face belonged to a connection I had been trying to connect with for the past year. Yes I said year. Multiple emails. Multiple phone calls to his office. And no response. No response for 365 days.

So I seized the moment to connect.

I grabbed my business card and I grabbed my phone.
Yes. I grabbed a business card. If you recall from earlier,
I use them sparingly if I'm in a fast-paced space and
place where there's no time to waste like speed networking or twerking. This definitely qualified as a
fast-paced space, so I grabbed my business card and
my phone.

From my phone I emailed the connection with the
subject line—greetings from the business fellowship
graduation. The body of the message said something
like this—it was great to meet you at the business
fellowship graduation...I would love to grab coffee in
the coming weeks to learn more about the great work
that you do, so please let me know the best way to get
on your calendar. Then I wrote the same message on
the back of my business card. The same exact message.
And the next moment moved fast and slow at the same
damn time. It was dreamlike. Slow motion. Slower
motion. Slowest motion. It was a rewind mixed with a
fast-forward. I wish it was recorded.

My row was on deck. We were up next to be called to
the stage, and just as fate would have it—I had to pass
his row to get to the stage! When I got to his row, I
noticed there was an empty seat next to him. I quickly
got out of the procession line, sat down next to him and
handed him my card. During the transaction, I introduced myself and recited the message. The same
message in the email. The same message on my business card. *"Hello, my name is Keisha Mabry and I've been
trying to connect with you for a year. I would love to grab*

coffee to discuss the great work that you do. Please let me know the best way to get on your calendar. By the way, I just emailed you too."

He was impressed, to say the least. He emailed me back immediately and cc'd his assistant to schedule time for us to meet. I shook his hand, thanked him for his time and quickly hopped back in the procession line. Everyone in the room looked at me super-geeked. *"Only Keish,"* a few of my fellow fellows squeaked.

5.69
Be An SME

What's a SME? A SME is a subject matter expert and it's something you should strive to be. Being a SME is a great way to meet peeps because when you are a SME people seek you out for your expertise. I've always been known for my connecting and socializing expertise, so when people seek resources, places to be and people to see—they seek me.

What subject, what matter and what expertise can you share with the world? Coaching, investing, exercising, training—the list goes on and on and on. So identify it, certify it and don't be quiet. Broadcast and share your SME everywhere. And I do mean everywhere. I share my SME on my social media, on my email signature and on my website. I speak, I teach, I give workshops and I even do retreats. Everybody I talk to knows my SME, and the more I spread the news, the more I get introduced.

5.70

Speak And Teach

If you're not scared to public speak. Speak. Find your stage and speak. I have made some cherished connections by speaking and teaching. From design weeks to meet and greets. I speak. From work to church. I speak. From associations to organizations. I speak. In short, if I have a membership. I speak. And speaking always leads to connectivity.

There are so many ways to speak, from stages to video conferencing. But—there's always a but—if the idea of speaking makes you feel like vomiting, get some speaker coaching before you hit the scene and bomb the thing. Programs like Toastmasters can help you develop public speaking skills in a safe and supportive space. So practice your umms, practice your pauses, practice your grace and practice your face before hitting the stage.

5.71

Talk TED

TED is a nonpartisan nonprofit devoted to spreading ideas in the form of short, powerful talks. TED began in 1984 as a conference where technology, entertainment and design converged, and today the talks cover almost everything. There are more than 2,200 TED talks, and one of these can be yours one day.

Nomination is very competitive—it's not easy—but think about the people you can connect with by speaking. I auditioned for a local TED talk this year and got rejected. RE-JEC-TED. But don't be sad. I only shed one tear. That one single celebrity tear. You know the one. If you don't, google BuzzFeed single tears shed and enjoy the fun.

Back to being REJECTED. That wasn't my first rejection and it won't be my last. I'll get my TED talk one day, so this rejection shall pass. On the bright side, the audition was really fun and I connected with a few-dozen audience members when I was done. So. I still won. You should try your hand at auditioning too, and much luck friend, I'm rooting for you.

5.72

Drop A Line

Make a new friend by dropping a line from time to time. I drop lines when people get promotions, when people get awards, when people graduate, when people join boards, when people get married and when people expand their family. If I don't personally know the person, I drop lines via social media. If I personally know the person, I drop lines via email, text, phone calls, cards and sticky notes. But regardless of the medium, the message is always the same—congrats on such and such.

I find this good news in various places and spaces: in newspapers, magazines, newsletters, social scenes, social media and word-of-mouth. Once I have the news, I drop at least two lines. I drop the initial line to say congrats, and I drop the second line a few weeks later to follow up and connect. In the second line, I say things like, *"How's the new job, or how's the new board? Let's connect soon—I would love to learn more about you and your new xyz. I'm available the week of xyz, so please let me know when you're free."*

P.S. Like dropping lines, you should also drop knowledge from time to time, like articles, resources, information and sources, because everyone has goals they are trying to reach and you can meet new peeps by helping them achieve.

5.73

Say Thanks

Back in the day, thank you notes weren't the exception to the rule—they were the rule. But not anymore. People rarely send or receive these, and when they do receive them, they are floored. Whether they get them via snail mail or email, they are surprised. Why? Because we've stopped saying thank you. Just like we've stopped saying hello. And you know what else? People don't dance NO MO. Yes. I said no mo.

What happened to dancing? What happened to pleasantry? What happened to Southern hospitality? Granted, my views are a bit skewed since I grew up in the Midwest. BUT I still believe this is one of the best ways to connect. There's just something about receiving handwritten stationery in the mail, and you don't have to be a Midwesterner or Southern Belle to send a handwritten letter in the mail.

Picture this. You move to a new city and your first week on the job you receive a handwritten note welcoming you to the city, thanking you for a previous meeting and wishing you the best, much luck and much success. And with the note there are flowers. You look at the sender expecting it to be your colleague, but it's not. It's a new friend you met for coffee a few days back.

Your next thought is *whoa, someone went slightly out of their way to wish me a good day.* But if you're anything like a lot of my friends, your next thought is that is *weird and a bit creepy.* Considering someone you just met a few days ago sent you flowers to your place of employment. But I thought it was the awesomest thing in the world, and six years later I'm still friends with that person today.

Now I'm not telling you to go around sending flowers and handwritten notes to everyone you meet. I say all of this to emphasize how powerful a handwritten note can be. Whether you are trying to connect with a client, colleague, future employer or mentor—handwritten notes are the way to go, so go. Go get you some thank you notes and start thanking folks.

5·74
Follow Up And Follow Through

Follow up, follow through and do what you said you were going to do. If you said you were going to email someone by such and such day, then get it done. If you said you were going to call someone for such and such reason, then get it done. If you said you were going to send someone such and such, then get it done. Do what you said you were going to do to connect with the peeps you want to get connected to.

You also want to follow up and follow through with folks that don't respond to you. **Note:** Not everyone is going to respond to you the first time you email them, if email is your method of contact to connect. I'm not sure how many emails you have sitting in your inbox, but I have 436. Yes. I said 436. Thinking about it makes me sick. Truly sick. And that's my work inbox. I have over 1,000 in my personal inbox, so both of my inboxes need a detox.

Is there a service for this? For cleaning out one's emails??? I would totally pay like today, so please let me know if there is. If not, someone please start this biz.

So no. Not everyone will respond to you the first time you email them, because they are swimming in emails and/or they have very busy lives themselves. With that said, don't fret if this happens to you. Just circle back in a week or two. I usually put a note in my calendar to circle back two weeks after I email somebody. And when I re-email them, I "respond all" to the previous email I sent and say:

Hello so-and-so,

I hope you are having a great week thus far.

Emailing to circle back to find some time to connect.

My schedule is pretty free on xyz, so please let me know the best way to get on your calendar. Looking forward to it!

KM

This usually works, but sometimes I have to email folks three times—and three times is where I usually draw the line. Then the person gets added to my circle-back-in-a-month-or-two list or my drop-a-line-from-time-to-time list. Yes. I have lists. In fact I have a CRM—a connection relationship management—strategy that I use, and I am currently developing a technology tool too, so be on the lookout, because it's coming soon!

5.75

Schedule Connection Time

The 21st century should be coined the century of the calendar. People schedule everything these days: date nights, exercise, lunch, brunch, vacation, meditation and even sleep. We schedule everything to maximize our time and to make time for the things that matter most. Well friend. I schedule connection time, because making connections matters to me. Making connections is important to me. And, therefore, making connections has a place on my calendar, schedule, agenda, planner, daytimer, diary—you name it.

Every month I schedule time to connect with people via phone, email and text. I schedule at least three days. One day to phone 3 to 5 people on my connection chart. One day to email 5 to 10 people on my connection chart. And one day to text 10 to 20 people on my connection chart. *"So what are you saying to these people?"* you're probably thinking.

Well friend it depends. Sometimes I am trying to arrange an in-person connection. Other times I am congratulating them on good news, sometimes I am sharing something of value and then there are times when I am just stopping by to say hi. The goal is to stay in touch, to stay top of mind and to not only curate new connections but to cultivate the ones I already have. So get to scheduling and get to connecting. You'll thank me later.

5.76

Be A Connector

Be a connector. Be a me. Be a person that introduces peeps to peeps. A person that introduces others to others that others should meet, and sooner than later people will return the favor. That's it. This way is that simple and that quick.

5.77

Connect Cold

A cold connection is a connection in which you reach out to a person that you don't know personally. Or even worse, you reach out to a person that doesn't know you personally. In a perfect world, cold connections are warmed by a third party. But as you probably already know from experiencing this thing called life—life isn't always perfect. Typically, I don't recommend this type of connecting, but sometimes this type of connecting is your only option. So if you cannot find anyone to make the introduction for you—try a cold connection…but make it appear warm.

Research the person, google them, link with them on LinkedIn, befriend them on Facebook, follow them on Twitter and read their social media feeds. Read as much as you can read and see as much as you can see. See if you can find an upcoming event the person is attending and accidently bump into them there. I like to call this a bump and talk. Not a bump and stalk but a bump and talk.

I did a bump and stalk, I mean talk, recently at a young professional summit I was attending. I was there to speak on a panel about connecting and branding and noticed a few weeks earlier that a person I had been dying to connect with was the keynote speaker for the event. So upon arriving, I planned out my seating. I sat in the V of the room. Not sure if you know about the V. But when I was in college, many professors told me that they teach and speak to the V of the classroom.

Imagine a classroom. Now imagine the professor's or speaker's point of view. Picture a V with the professor or speaker standing at the open end of the V and her/his vantage point ending in the back of the room where the two ends meet. That's the V and that's the area of the room most professors and speakers draw their attention to and speak to.

So I sat in the V and I sat in a seat that made it easy for me to leave. It worked like a charm. The speaker made eye contact with me multiple times during his speech. As I expected, he made a beeline for the door after his keynote and I was close by in tow. He looked at me as soon as I opened the door and said, *"Don't I know you?"* I responded and said, *"Yes and no. We have never met officially, but we have seen each other out and about a few times."* He extended his hand, we introduced ourselves "officially" and he agreed to meet with me over coffee. And that my friend is a bump and talk in action.

If you can't bump and talk, try to find a commonality. An association, organization, board, camp, club, church, cohort, college, colleague, fellowship, conference, family member, fraternity, sorority, friend, hobby, mastermind, mentor, sport or travel group and use this common interest to turn a cold connection warm. Then send the person an email or a direct message with the commonality in the subject line like this—greetings from United Way. In the body of the message, be specific about the purpose of your outreach and make sure they know why you want to meet.

I repeat. Make sure they know why you want to meet. Do you want to hear their story, do you want to hear their expertise, do you want to collaborate or do you want a roommate? Seriously. Why do you want to meet? You should know this and they should too.

The other thing you should know is your value. What value can you provide them in return for their time, their expertise and their willingness to meet? Remember, connecting isn't a one-way street—it's a two-way street. It's reciprocal. It's give-give-give and take. Not take-take-take and give. I repeat. Connecting isn't a one-way street—it's a two-way street. It's reciprocal. It's give-give-give and take. Not take-take-take and give.

All right friend? Ok. Ok. I'm done preaching. I'll let you live. So now that you know, start connecting cold and feel free to use my guide below.

Subject: *Greetings from United Way*

Hello Kim,

I received your contact information at the United Way Young Friends' event last week. I was talking to a young friend of the board and she felt we should meet.

I work at The Connection Curator, a connection agency with ONE GOAL—*"change the world one connection at a time." We are a group of wooers, doers and social influencers committed to connecting people to people and people to resources.*

We believe young professionals need more opportunities to mix and mingle, and we heard you believe this to be true too! We would like to partner with you to roll out a series of connection events for young professionals in the metro area. We have a ton of ideas in mind, as well as the capacity and time to organize and execute.

My schedule is pretty flexible the week of the 8th and 16th, so please let me know what works best for you. Looking forward to it!

KM

Part Six: Use Tech

Social media and technology are great ways to meet peeps because they are oh so quick and easy. But, and this is a huge BUT, the goal is to use social media as a tool to stimulate in-person connections, not as a tool to substitute them.

6.78

Be Googlable

Have you googled yourself lately? You should google yourself daily. Ok. Ok. Daily may be a little excessive, but google yourself at least monthly. You want to know what Google has to say about you. You want to know if you're googlable.

Why? Because people are stalkerish nowadays. As soon as people meet you in person or hear your name, they generally do two things. 1. They google you. 2. They link with you on LinkedIn. So again, are you googlable?

If not, start building your Google presence ASAP. Get a personal website, get on LinkedIn, get on Twitter, get on boards and get awards. Get googlable because Google can make or break your future connections.

6.79

Hire PR

Everything you do is an opportunity for people to connect with you, BUT not everything you do has to be done by you. Platforms like Fiverr.com and Upwork.com make it easy and affordable to hire freelance work. I've hired many freelance folks to help me with branding, exposure and PR-related things. I've even hired my friends.

Freelancers have designed social media videos for me, they had edited content like articles and posts, they have developed items for my website, and their help makes it easier for me to sleep at night. What can a freelancer take off your plate? For a good rate, you can get the help you need to get googlable, connect with more peeps and get more sleep.

6.80

Get Linked

Get linked on LinkedIn and Facebook too! And don't just create a profile—join several groups!!! Groups give you instant access to a group of people that share similar interests with you and provide you a quick and easy way to connect. All you have to do is simply like, share, comment and share content. And when people like, share, comment and share content back, be sure to interact.

I recently joined a Facebook group with 3 million members. I posted a picture on the group's wall and received more than 500 likes and reactions in the first hour. Wowzers. I think it was my blue pantsuit. Yes I actually wore a pantsuit, but it was a makeshift pantsuit, so technically it wasn't a suit but any who...I was cute and I was rocking my spring statement shoes. Many people commented and in true fashion I responded. Then a lady acknowledged that we went to the same college. And just like that I made another connection.

P.S. Twitter has groups too, but they are called lists. I haven't quite figured out how these work just yet, so I'll keep my two cents.

P.P.S. In addition to the usual suspects, there are

other social media sites too, like—deep breath—Instagram, YouTube, Pinterest, Periscope, Google+, Tumblr, Reddit, Flickr, Vine, Meetup, Musical.ly, Ask, WhatsApp, Slack, Classmates, Foursquare, WeChat and Snapchat. All of which can be used to connect.

6.81

Get GroupMe

There's a GroupMe for everything just like there's a Facebook group for everything. So find GroupMe's you can join or GroupMe's you can form. I'm in a few too many: a family GroupMe, a young professional GroupMe, a women in entrepreneurship GroupMe, a business diversity initiative GroupMe, a girls' night out GroupMe, a mastermind GroupMe, a sorority GroupMe, a friends that travel GroupMe and many, many, many more. Unlike Facebook groups, GroupMe's are harder to find but definitely worth the time. They allow you to connect with several folks at once, so ear hustle, eavesdrop, snoop, pry, spy and meddle your way to some.

6.82

Look For LISTSERVS

Like GroupMe, there's a LISTSERV for everything and I'm on one too many of those too. More like 10 too many. But I love LISTSERVS. They keep you in the loop and lucky for you, some people still show the emails too! Yes that's right. Instead of using databases like MailChimp and Constant Contact, they just cc everyone, and these are my favorite ones. When I see these types of LISTSERVS, I feel like I've hit the jackpot. Then I plot. I plot my connection plan and I scan.

I scan the email addresses and I look for familiar names. First names, last names and company names. I look for people on my connection chart and use the LISTSERV as a way to start conversation. It's a great excuse, because the people on the LISTSERV have at least one thing in common with you—the purpose of the LISTSERV itself—so you can email them without being stealth.

Here's how. 1. You can connect by simply replying to emails sent via the LISTSERV. Be sure to keep the subject line the same and be sure to direct your response to the person or persons you want to connect with. 2. You can also connect by emailing the person or persons with the subject line—greetings from xyz LISTSERV. Like connecting cold, it's important for you to be specific about the purpose of your outreach in the body of the email. Make sure they know why you want to meet and state it clearly.

On the flip side, if none of the names on the LISTSERV look familiar—google them like I do. I'm sure this may sound a bit stalkerish to you, but you never know who may be one degree of separation away from you. The names are there, right there, so have a looksee and see who you can meet.

Lastly, sometimes LISTSERVS hide the personal emails of their peeps, but they allow you to see the email address for the LISTSERV itself. With this LISTSERV address, you can simply connect with peeps by emailing the email addy…but not all LISTSERVS have this functionality.

6.83

Be A Guest

Events happen monthly, weekly, daily and hourly. Events happen when it's sunny and when it's cloudy. Events happen. And some are peaceful and some are rowdy. Events happen. And when events happen, guests are invited, old friends are reunited and new friends are united. But before events can happen, guest lists have to be formed and folks have to be informed.

When hosts invite guests, they have one goal—attendance. To get the people they invite to attend. As a guest, you should have a goal too—connections. To attend the event and connect with as many guests as you can.

However, your connections do not have to begin at the event. Your connections can begin as soon as the invitation is sent. Hosts have multiple invite tools they can choose and use, like Evite, Eventbrite, Paperless Post and Punchbowl. When hosts use these tools, sometimes they make the guest lists visible for you to view.

When you have visibility, you can simply message other guests through the tool or post a message on the event wall. And your message doesn't have to be big…it can be small. A small invite of your own to say how much you're looking forward to having some fun and meeting everyone.

You can even reach out to folks attending events you don't attend. Weird but true. I do it all the time. Well. That's a stretch. Maybe not all of the time, but I've done it a few times. If there's an event I really want to attend but can't attend in the end, I will email guests or message them on social media with the subject line— greetings from xyz event.

In the body of the email, I will introduce myself and state that I was really looking forward to meeting them at xyz event but ended up being unable to attend. Then I will propose a meeting over coffee, and a date and space to discuss xyz. Sometimes it works. Sometimes it don't. Sometimes it will. Sometimes it won't. But it's well worth a try.

6.84

Take Pictures

I hate taking pictures. I know I'm not supposed to say the word hate—sorry Mom—but I hate taking pictures. Yet you would never know, because I take pictures every day. Every single day. Why? Pics or it didn't happen. And this isn't just a meme—it's a belief. If you don't take pictures these days and if you don't post pictures these days, IT DID NOT HAPPEN. I repeat. IT DID NOT HAPPEN.

I take pictures on my own with my phone and I take pictures at events. Most events have at least one photographer. At least one paparazzo. At least one camera-man or woman. And I used to run from these shutter-bugs, but now I run to them.

I run to them, because it's free press and free press can lead to multiple opportunities to connect. Pictures can end up on walls, in blogs, in magazines and in social media feeds. Pictures can lead people to you and they have for me frequently, so dress fly friend and smile or smize for the camera guy or gal. All right pal?

6.85
Tag People

Tag you're it. Sound familiar? Tag was one of my favorite, and I do mean favorite, games as a child but this isn't the tag I am speaking of. I am speaking of photo tags. People love taking pictures these days, so take pictures and tag away. And even for those that hate taking pictures—like me—there's something special about posting pictures and seeing what others think. So tag away. BUT. Only tag peeps that are in the pic because peeps hate getting tagged in pics they're not in!

When you tag people in pictures on social media, you not only get exposure from your connections, you also get exposure from their connections. Additionally, you can tag places by checking in and adding a location. This exposes you and your picture to other people that check into the same location and creates opportunities to reflect and connect.

So yes. Tagging works.

Please don't judge me but one time, maybe two or three, I made new connections when I checked in at Fatburger. And another time when I checked in at In-N-Out Burger. Yes I like good and cheap eats from time to time and yes I'm a poultritarian slash flexitarian, but that's not the point. The point of this matter is—the more you tag and the more you check in, the more friends you can connect with. So tag you're it.

6.86

Record A Video

It's no secret that we live in a microwave society. People want things fast and things change fast, especially technology. I just told you to take pictures, but with Facebook Live, Snapchat, Instagram Stories and camera 360s, one can be led to believe that pictures are becoming obsolete. I seriously doubt pictures will ever go away, but people like videos these days.

All you need is one viral video and you're set. You can be the next online sensation waiting to happen. I haven't accomplished viral video status yet, but I have had a video get 1,000 views and you can too! You can probably get more than me so try and see. My video is called Bandaid and it's a play on Beyoncé's Lemonade. Go check it out on my Facebook page!!! But to find it, you may be scrolling for days.

6.87

Do A Challenge

There is no shortage of challenges nowadays. In fact there's an abundance. There's the you name it challenge, the mannequin challenge, the running man challenge, the ice bucket challenge, the dub challenge, the Chuck E. Cheese challenge and the wedgie in my booty challenge. Yes friend. There's a challenge called the wedgie in my booty challenge. Just ask any teen or tween ages 10 to 15 and they should know all about it.

Challenges are engaging and entertaining connection opportunities. You can do one challenge or two. You can do a challenge solo or as a group. You can join in on an existing challenge or you can even create your own. And depending on when you're reading this book—some of these challenges may be long gone. Long, long gone so search the net for current ones.

Recently I created a connection challenge. It was a 7-day challenge with one goal—to get people to connect with as many people as they could in seven days.

Here were the rules:

1. *Follow me on Twitter **@KeishaMabry**.*

2. *Connect with as many people as you can connect with from October 24th to October 31st.*

3. *Take an usie every time you connect with someone and post the pic to your Twitter feed. Be sure to @KeishaMabry and use the hashtags #heyfriend, #friendworking and #100in100in100 in every pic.*

4. *That's it. It's as simple as 123 and the winner with the most connection usies will be announced on my social media feeds on Novmber 1st.*

This one 7-day challenge reached thousands of peeps on Facebook, Twitter and LinkedIn. I posted different messages to my social media feeds daily to advertise the challenge. I also purchased a $25 ad with Facebook and another $25 ad with Twitter to boost visibility. Lastly, I gave a $100 cash prize to the winner.

All of this activity led to 50 in-person connections, more than 250 new followers on LinkedIn, Twitter and Facebook, a few speaking engagements and hundreds of hits and visits to my personal website. I even picked up a feature in a magazine, two new coaching clients and three new book signings.

The silver lining. Challenges can be challenging whether you participate in an existing one or create your own. They require time, they require commitment and sometimes they require a picture or video to fulfill them. But they are well worth all of the above because you can get mad love, be a part of a viral trend and gain a lot of new friends.

6.88

Create Content

Content creators and curators are favored by many because they make our lives easy. When searching for recipes, home remedies and diagnosing ourselves on Wed MD—they make our lives easy. When looking for hairstyles, lifestyles, outfits and ChapStick—they make our lives easy. And content can be created fairly easy too.

USE TECH Content can be created for articles, blogs, journals and vlogs, newsletters, magazines and books—to name a few. Content can be created for work and content can be created for hobbies too. In short, content can be created for anything you want to, so find a niche and get hitched and stop being sluggish and get published.

6.89

Be An Influencer

Social media and online communities are always looking for influencers from LinkedIn to Yelp to Instagram, but the key here is consistency. Like content creators, influencers are peeps known for something: shopping, sipping, shipping or sight-seeing. They know what's hot and what's not. The social scene. The next big thing. The latest and greatest. The happenings. They got the juice, the keys and they know it all as it pertains to their one thing.

But influencers post regularly. Content creators can publish one-offs and two-offs, but not influencers. Influencers are regular contributors and distributors of content. Sometimes you can apply for these roles by submitting an online application, but most times someone else puts your name in rotation. That some-one else can be an editor, recruiter or agent, depending on the eliteness of the content's location. So as you can imagine, influencer jobs can be hard to get but well worth the connections.

I have a few friends that are influencers. A few are Twitter and Facebook influencers. Others are Yelp and LinkedIn influencers and then some are influencers for online communities like I Don't Do Clubs and Blavity. I am none of the above because I suck at consistency and, as mentioned above, influencers have to post frequently. Really daily if you ask me. And not just once a day but five to seven times a day.

Friend you can do this but you have to be true to this. So if you suck at consistency like me, you may need to hire someone to post for you or use a tool like Klout or Hootsuite. Capisce?

6.90
Send A Survey

With Google Forms, you can administer a survey, plan an event and collect data stress-free. You can also use Google Forms to connect peeps to peeps. Here are the deets.

When I attend events, I try to buy or get the guest list ahead of time. Like way ahead of time. Like three to four weeks if I can. Then I pre-plan. I call and email the attendees I want to connect with in advance. Then I wait. I wait for the calls and emails to trickle in. Some call and email me back instantly while others take their sweet precious time. Then there's folks that totally decline my invitation to meet. But for every no there's always a yes, and those are the best.

I meet with some yeses at breakfast, some at lunch, some for dinner and some for brunch. I meet with some during breaks, some during workshops, some in the shuttle and some during happy hour bar hops. The goal is to pre-plan and meet with as many peeps as possible, but that isn't always plausible.

If I can't buy or get the attendee list ahead of time, I search for attendees online. I scour the event's website, the event's social media feeds and the event's mobile app to find any and all attendees. Sometimes I strike gold and sometimes I come up empty. Sometimes I meet a few peeps and sometimes I meet plenty. Sometimes I work the room and schmooze with everyone I want to see, but a lot of times there's a ton of peeps I never get to meet.

That's when Google comes in.

To connect with more folks, I create a Google Form with the following fields: name, occupation, website, email address, Facebook handle, Twitter handle and anything else you want us to know. Then I post a link to the form on the event's social media pages with the following note, the official event hashtag and an @ to the event host:

> *There are so many peeps I need to meet and I'm sure you feel the same way too, so I created a Google Form to make connecting easier to do. Please visit the link below to share your contact info, and in three days I'll send the list to everyone that adds their info. Pass the word!*

A few weeks ago I attended a women's empowerment conference, and everyone in the room was DOPE. And I do mean everyone. I pre-planned my connections, I worked the room and I still didn't meet everyone I wanted to meet. So. Before leaving the conference, I created a Google Form. Then I hopped on the event's Facebook page, hopped on my Twitter page, posted the note above and got nothing but LOVE. People were commenting and sharing my link, and within minutes my form had the contact information for 50+ DOPE peeps.

6.91

Follow Followers

Games and clichés tell you to follow the leader, but I'm telling you to follow the follower. Ideally I want you to follow both. I use this way a lot on Twitter, LinkedIn, Facebook and Instagram. I look for influencers interested in topics that interest me, and I follow them. Then I follow their followers. I also follow friends of friends too. Most folks follow me back and when they do, I try to connect.

I initiate conversation by thanking them for the follow. Sometimes this leads to more conversation and then an in-person meeting if there's synergy and we live in the same city. Other times it leads to nothing and that's ok too, so don't let a non-follow get to you. If you want, you can un-follow the non-follower within a few weeks. There are apps that can help you do this quite easily.

So follow followers and watch who follows back, then initiate conversation and get some connects.

6.92

Follow Family

As of late I have been having a strong desire to find my family. In other words, I have been tracking down everyone that bears my last name, and social media has been my friend to this end. On Facebook I search my last name every few weeks and I always find new people to meet. I have come across family in my city and family on each coast. I have come across a Mabry Facebook group and family that are troops.

I have chatted with folks online, I have chatted with folks on the phone and I have even scheduled time to connect with those in cities I frequent most. It's been an amazing journey, and you can do it too. Just search your last name on Facebook and Google. Not everyone you meet will be your family per se, but it's still cool to connect with those who bear your last name.

6.93

Use Hashtags

By the dictionary's definition, hashtags are words or phrases used to categorize posts on a specific topic. By my definition, hashtags are words or phrases used to meet peeps because hashtags do one thing very well—they create a commonality. Whether you are a foodie, somewhat goofy, a globetrotter or into Harry Potter—

there's a hashtag for you and a community that shares that interest too.

On Twitter, your hashtags are limited by the character limits of the tweet. The more you speak in the tweet, the less hashtags you can keep. My Twitter hashtags are usually reflective of the event I am attending, but you can hashtag anything: news, concerts, cities and recipes, quotes, jokes, dares and footwear.

My personal goal is to tweet 50 tweets per event and to use the official event's hashtag in every tweet. Yes. I said 50. I tweet 100 at some events. The more you tweet, the more people you can meet. So tweet. Tweet pictures of speakers, pictures of food, pictures of new friends and pictures of you doing the event things that event people do. Tweet speaker quotes, tweet jokes, tweet thoughts and things you bought. Just tweet. Any and everything.

I tweet at conferences, at festivals, at ceremonies, at matrimonies, at workshops and at bar hops. You name it. I tweet at it and have started many Twitter conversations over my hashtag use. I comment, others comment and we connect. But for me, my goal is 'to not only' connect with people in social media space, my goal is 'to also' connect with people in person at the event place. So when I tweet-connect I will ask the person to meet me in person if I feel energy, chemistry and synergy.

My meetups vary by the event type, but I mainly tweet and meet at conferences. Sometimes I meet people for coffee before a conference session. Other times I meet people in the session and will save them a seat to sit with me. Sometimes I meet people for breakfast, lunch, dinner or dunch. And other times I meet people for a cocktail at the conference bar. But regardless, I never go far.

I am always on the safer side when meeting people in person for the first time—even at conferences. I always meet people in a safe space at a safe place on conference property. I repeat. I always meet people in a safe space at a safe place on conference property. So obey this rule okay, because safety is not the exception—it's the rule.

When I am not tweeting at an event, I usually tweet about connecting, friendworking, education, innovation, entrepreneurship, current events and other things of interest. Or. I tweet about trending hashtags on Twitter, and there are various ways to find this info. 1. You can simply start a new tweet. If you type the hashtag symbol, a list of the top hashtags for that day will populate. 2. You can visit websites like Hashtagify. me and Hashtags.org, or you can follow these websites on Twitter to get the latest and greatest hashtag news! You choose.

On Instagram, you can post 30 hashtags per picture. And if you were wondering—I post 30 hashtags per picture. I really do. For every picture. Every single picture. My favorites are *#friend, #potd, #qotd, #igdaily, #instadaily, #like, #love, #mood, #travel, #fashion and #photography*. But, like Twitter, you can find the top Instagram hashtags for any given day on websites like Top-Hashtags.org, Tophashtags.net and Instagramtags.com.

Note: Hashtag websites tend to look a little sketch.

I don't believe they have malware, but I am not 100% sure, so beware. Also beware that some people hate when people post more than two to three hashtags per pic. They will even try to call you out on it. They will even call you thirsty. But friend, you can't live life worried about what others think and say. Hashtags foster connecting, so hashtag away.

On Facebook, I rarely use hashtags, so I'm probably missing out on some really great connects. But when I do use hashtags, I tend to follow trends, and of course I use my hashtags **#friendworking** and **#heyfriend**. To find trending topics on Facebook, it's pretty simple. Just scan your news feed or click on the search bar while in the app. Then scroll to the bottom of the page and give the trending hashtags a tap.
Happy hashtagging!

6.94
Search Hashtags

You're probably thinking there's another hashtag way. Yes friend. You're going to learn today. Searching hashtags has been the start of many friendships for me. But when I say search hashtags, I don't want you to search for trends. I want you to search for things that interest you, like *#heyfriend*, the latest *#cleanse* and the best *#pens*. I want you to search. Then I want you to befriend new friends.

Another way to use this way is for events you attend or events you want to attend but can't. By searching hashtags, you can connect with people while at the event, after the event and even in your absence. Just locate the official hashtag for the event, experience or incident and search away. Search your way to a new friend to befriend and, if you can, try to connect with them in person.

6.95

Retweet Tweets

Now that you're a hashtag pro, here's another way to flow you to folks. Retweets. Yes friend, retweets. It's not a retwit but a retweet, and retweets get you connected to peeps.

Twitter has more than 300 million monthly active users. 300 million a month. Crazy huh? And these 300 million a month users are always on the hunt to get more followers, and one trick to do this is to retweet tweets.

When you retweet tweets, people will do one of three things. **1.** They will look at your profile. **2.** They will retweet the same tweet. **3.** They will follow you if the tweet you retweeted was their tweet. Or. They will follow you if they want you to follow them back. Or. They will follow you if they want to know more about the peep behind the retweet. So retweets work. But before you start your retweeting spurt, you may need to rework your profile first.

QUESTION.

Is your profile dated or updated? Does it catch peoples' eyes or do they scroll on by? Do you have a headshot and a backdrop? Do you have a good bio or does it blow? In other words, is your profile wack or does it have swag?

Know before you go on a retweeting spree by checking out profiles of other peeps. Start by checking out the profiles of influencers. They are the peeps with the blue checkmarks next to their names. Benchmark their profiles to get ideas for your own. Then hone in on what you want and should post. Then post. Update your profile and post. Post and retweet as many tweets as you can and land you some new friends.

6.96
Tweet Chat

A tweet chat is a live Twitter conversation around one distinct hashtag. They're usually hosted by a specific person or organization and are open to the public. Anyone can participate by tweeting a response to the question(s) posed by the host and by using the distinct hashtag in their post. Like popular hashtags, there are websites one can use to find the date and time of various chats. Or. One can simply search "tweet chat" in the search bar on Twitter. Or. One can be voluntold.

I've been voluntold for two tweet chats and those tweets came back to back to back. My first tweet chat almost gave me an anxiety attack. I'm exaggerating but not by much. It was definitely a rush but a good rush.

Both tweet chats were centered around education. Around getting students the tools they could use to successfully transition from high school to college.

Around sharing knowledge for a good cause. Around laws that help and hurt students from lower socio-economic backgrounds and sound advice to help them out.

USE TECH The tweet chat started at a certain time and all of us involved hopped online. Prior to the chat, we were all given a pack of questions and from those questions we were able to think through our suggestions. This made it a tad bit easier to keep up with the chat, but those questions still came back to back to back. And not only did we have to answer questions from the moderator, we also had to answer questions posed by students, parents and educators.

The chat lasted an hour, but it felt like forever; however, I met dozens of new peeps from this superb social effort. I met dozens of new students and dozens of new parents, dozens of new educators and dozens of new legislators. I met so many cool peeps from New York to The Bay, and many of us still talk today. So tweet away, meet away and when you become a tweet chat pro, be sure to organize your own.

6.97

Podcast

Have you heard of Serial? Not cereal (c.e.r.e.a.l.) but Serial (s.e.r.i.a.l.). It's a podcast that has been downloaded and streamed more than 5 million times on iTunes. 5 MILLION TIMES. And guess why it's so popular? Because it tells stories. That's it. Stories. This podcast connects with millions of people weekly by sharing a story.

So are you ready to share your story? Are you ready to connect with millions of peeps? Try podcasting. It's free and it's easy. Well, almost free. It takes time and a minimum investment in equipment. Need a blueprint? Well. You need a mic, a laptop or cell, recording software and a hosting site. If you still have no clue of what to do—go to YesYouCanPodcastToo.com.

I just started my own podcast called The Connection Club, and I had 100 downloads within the first 24 hours. Talk about connection power, and for my podcast I use the following tools:

- *Mic: Audio-Technica ATR 2100*
- *Laptop: MacBook Pro*
- *Recording Software: Audacity*
- *Hosting Site: Libsyn*
- *Posting Sites: iTunes, Google Play and Sound Cloud*

I record at home, but many libraries and universities have free recording equipment and space you can use. There are even podcast studios where you can record too, but it'll cost you. The cost typically includes a podcast producer and a sound engineer that will edit and post your audio files too. But I will warn you. Podcasting is a time commitment, and your episodes need to be consistent. Your niche needs to be specific, your sound needs to be terrific and your episodes need to be prolific to get a grand following.

Unfortunately, my podcast was none of the above.

Well, a few were, but it wasn't consistent. My travel schedule made it difficult to maintain it and it tanked. I did really great for three weeks, then I fell off and my followers did too. I am hoping to get up and running again in the new year once this book is done. It was a ton of fun and an awesome way to connect, but I just wasn't ready yet. So be ready before you start, and please record at least five episodes before you go live.

Part Seven:
Get Extra Credit

I'm a former teacher and an over-achiever, so extra credit is always to be expected. But here's the catch. The ways that follow are extra ways you can use to meet more peeps, but I haven't personally used them yet. However, I have seen them used and they seem to work well, so try your hand at them, beaus and belles.

7.98

Buy Coffee

EXTRA
CREDIT

A few months back, I came across a website entitled Free Coffee With Aubrey. The title intrigued me so I clicked to learn all about it, see all about it and read all about it. I'm glad I did, because Aubrey was cool peeps and Aubrey was just like you and me—she was a transitional looking for connection opportunities.

Aubrey was new to the Lou. She moved and didn't know a soul but she did have a goal—meet new peeps over coffee, and that's exactly what she did. Aubrey started her connection journey by building a website. Then. She shared her website on social media with the following note, *"I'd like to buy you a cup of Joe so submit a request below. You choose the shop, I buy the cup and then I will write a blog about you!"* As you can imagine and probably guess, people started signing up right and left.

I mean. Who doesn't like freebies? Free press and free coffee? Sign me up please.

On average, Aubrey purchased a cup of Joe for 1 to 3 new folks a month, and over the course of three years Aubrey met more than 92 new friends. And yes friend. I had coffee with Aubrey. You too can use coffee as a connection tool. Visit Aubrey's website at www.freecoffeewithaubrey.com to learn more about this way and offer to buy someone a cup of coffee today.

7.99

Lounge In The Library

With the increase in e-books and audio books, libraries are becoming obsolete and extinct, but they are still important to our communities. Libraries are gathering places and libraries are safe spaces. But above all, libraries provide ample opportunities to meet new faces.

EXTRA CREDIT

Unbeknownst to me, libraries offer more than racks of hardbacks and paperbacks. Libraries have 3D printing and various trainings, art exhibits and film installations, wifi and recording lessons, makerspaces and speaker sessions, story-times and book clubs for FREE99. Yes you heard me. All of these things are free, and all of these things generate opportunities to meet peeps, so frequent your local library and meet, meet, meet.

7.100

Start A Show

What's your SSB? You know. Your SSB. Your secret single behavior. We all have them. Sometimes we share them and sometimes we don't, but we all have them. Carrie from Sex in the City used to eat jelly on saltines and read fashion magazines when home and alone. Miranda used to put Vaseline on her hands and watch infomercials, while Charlotte examined her pores in a magnifying mirror. Samantha didn't have any SSB's, which is hard to believe, but I do. I do and I'm sure you do too. So what do you do? What do you do when home and alone?

I pretend I have a show. That's right. A show. Sometimes it's a reality show, sometimes it's a comedy show and other times it's a fashion show. Sometimes it takes place in the living room, sometimes it takes place in the bathroom and other times it takes place in the kitchen. Regardless, my show is the biz-ness.

I do everything from performing standup comedy and improv acts, to trying on clothes and strutting my stuff up and down the hallway like a runway. I even pose in the bathroom mirror to fake camera snaps, I sing, I rap and I even act. Oh how I act. I do voiceovers for fake cartoons and dramatic scenes for fake romantic comedies. I do it all. I even recite poetry.

I become the star of my own show and she becomes me—but we become a we in theory. Yes. I said in theory, not reality. My secret single behavior show is a theory because no one knows about my show but me. I often wish I was on someone's TV, but right now no one knows about my show but me.

Unlike me, many have used their secret single behaviors to start their own shows. Real shows. Not shows in theory but shows in reality. Shows that others other than themselves see. And this can be you and me.

You can connect with others by being the star of your own show. By recording your secret single behavior on your camera or phone, editing it with apps and software like iMovie and Final Cut and uploading it to YouTube for others to see. And in addition to your secret single behavior, you can record other content too, like product reviews, TV show reviews, tutorial how-to's and top celebrity news. Then you can create a YouTube channel to keep all of your shows in one spot, and if your shows are any good, new friends and new followers will start to flock.

The End

Well friend. We've come to the end, but this is the book that never ends. Kind of like Lamb Chop's Play-Along, this is The Song That Doesn't End. I used to sing that song just to aggravate my brother, and it worked. I was such a jerk. But you don't have to be. You don't have to be a networking jerk. You now have 100 ways to connect with 100 people in 100 days. But the keyword here is connect. Don't network. Connect. Share your story, share your who and connect like I've taught you to.

In Friendship,

KEISHA

A Special Thanks to My Friends

I would like to take a moment to thank the following friends for their features in my book. And yes, we are friends—some of them just don't know it yet.

Beyoncé
Ca$h Out
Dave Chappelle
Drake
Janelle Monáe
Jodie Sweetin
Kanye West
Kevin Hart
Lil Scrappy
Lil Wayne
Mike Epps
Rihanna
T-Pain
Tyra Banks
Usher

A special thanks to the late and great Bernie Mac, Biggie Smalls, Fred McFeely Rogers, Nelson Mandela, Rick James and Zig Ziglar too – may their memories live on.

Citations

Betz A (n.d.): *St. Louisans I've Met.* Retrieved December 15, 2016, from www.freecoffeewithaubrey.com

Coleman HJ: *Empowering Yourself: The Organizational Game Revealed.* Dubuque, Iowa, 1996, Kendall/Hunt Pub.

Ferrazzi K and Raz T: *Never Eat Alone: And Other Secrets to Success, One Relationship at a Time.* New York, 2014, Crown Business.

Liu J: *"Nones" On the Rise.* Retrieved November 30, 2016, from www.pewforum.org/2012/10/09/nones-on-the-rise

Rhimes S: *Year of Yes.* New York, 2015, Simon & Schuster.

Star D (Writer): *The Good Fight* [television series episode, 2002, January 6]. In *Sex and the City.* New York, New York: HBO.

ABOUT THE AUTHOR

Keisha Mabry is a friendworking friend-spret (friendship expert) who travels the world teaching people how to make friends everywhere. And when we say everywhere, we do mean everywhere. On planes, on trains, in lines and while she dines!

Keisha's #friendworking philosophy is routed in the who of the person, not the do of the person. Who they are versus what they do for a living. It's story sharing and people caring, and Keisha's been friend-working for more than 10 years. She starts every conversation the same, what's your story, and will teach you how to do it too—100 ways with 100 people in 100 days. Starting today!

New you, new goal, new grad, new role, new startup, new state, new career, new mate? Connect with 100 people in 100 days to feel zen, get in, earn wins and make friends!

P.S. *Keisha is on LinkedIn, Facebook and Twitter @KeishaMabry.*